CAMBRIDGE SCHOOL

Shakespeare

King Richard II

Edited by Michael Clamp

Series Editor: Rex Gibson
Director, Shakespeare and Schools Project

Published by the Press Syndicate of the University of Cambridge
The Pitt Building, Trumpington Street, Cambridge CB2 1RP
40 West 20th Street, New York, NY 10011–4211, USA
10 Stamford Road, Oakleigh, Victoria 3166, Australia

First published 1992

Printed in Great Britain at the University Press, Cambridge

British Library cataloguing in publication data
Shakespeare, William *1564–1616*
King Richard II. – (Cambridge School Shakespeare).
1. English drama
I. Title II. Clamp, Michael
822.33

Library of Congress cataloguing in publication data applied for

ISBN 0 521 40946 2 paperback

Designed by Richard Morris
Illustrations by Jones and Sewell Associates
Picture research by Callie Kendall

Acknowledgements

Jacket, p. 92: by courtesy of The Dean and Chapter of Westminster; 16*l*, Reg Wilson; 16*c*, 186, National Portrait Gallery, London; 16*r*, Hulton Picture Company; 20, Graphische Sammlung Albertina, Vienna; 22, 116, 193*b*, by permission of the British Library; 28, Mander and Mitcheson Theatre Collection; 52, 114, 128, 138, 142, 172, Donald Cooper; 64, National Gallery, London; 68, Cliché des Musées Nationaux, Paris/Musée de Cluny; 74, Shakespeare Centre Library, Stratford-upon-Avon/Gordon Goode; 84, Tapisserie de Bayeux et avec autorisation spéciale de la Ville de Bayeux; 88, Bridgeman Art Library/by permission of the British Library; 98, courtesy of Rex Gibson; 136, 185, Joe Cocks Studio; 154, Bridgeman Art Library/courtesy of the Trustees of the British Museum; 193, reproduced by permission of the Board of Trustees of the Victoria & Albert Museum

Contents

Cambridge School Shakespeare

This edition of *King Richard II* is part of the *Cambridge School Shakespeare* series. Like every other play in the series, it has been specially prepared to help all students in schools and colleges.

This *King Richard II* aims to be different from other editions of the play. It invites you to bring the play to life in your classroom, hall or drama studio through enjoyable activities that will increase your understanding. Actors have created their different interpretations of the play over the centuries. Similarly, you are encouraged to make up your own mind about *King Richard II*, rather than having someone else's interpretation handed down to you.

Cambridge School Shakespeare does not offer you a cut-down or simplified version of the play. This is Shakespeare's language, filled with imaginative possibilities. To help you explore all aspects of these possibilities, you will find on every left-hand page: a summary of the action, an explanation of unfamiliar words, a choice of activities on Shakespeare's language, characters and stories.

Between each act and in the pages at the end of the play, you will find notes, illustrations and activities. These will help to increase your understanding of the whole play.

There are a large number of activities to give you the widest choice to suit your own particular needs. Please don't think you have to do every one. Choose the activities that will help you most.

This edition will be of value to you whether you are studying for an examination, reading for pleasure, or thinking of putting on the play to entertain others. You can work on the activities on your own or in groups. Many of the activities suggest a particular group size, but don't be afraid to make up larger or smaller groups to suit your own purposes.

Although you are invited to treat *King Richard II* as a play, you don't need special dramatic or theatrical skills to do the activities. By choosing your activities, and by exploring and experimenting, you can make your own interpretations of Shakespeare's language, characters and stories. Whatever you do, remember that Shakespeare wrote his plays to be acted, watched and enjoyed.

Rex Gibson

This edition of *King Richard II* uses the text of the play established by Andrew Gurr in *The New Cambridge Shakespeare*.

Where does the play begin?

The origins of the struggle between King Richard II and Henry Bullingbrook, Duke of Hereford, the man who seized his throne, lie further back in history than the quarrel between Bullingbrook and Thomas Mowbray, Duke of Norfolk, which begins the play. Behind this dispute between the two great lords lies a whole series of political moves and counter-moves in the centuries-long struggle for power between the medieval king and his nobles.

King Richard, at this point in his reign (April 1398), was at the height of his royal powers, perhaps more powerful than any feudal king of England before him. Yet it had not always been so. In 1388, five powerful lords (called the Lords Appellant) had set about removing the King's advisers and taking control of government. There was even some talk of deposing the king, but they could not agree amongst themselves about who should succeed him. Richard had to watch helplessly as his friends and supporters were accused, imprisoned and executed.

But Richard knew how to bide his time. While the Lords Appellant took over the reins of government, Richard quietly set about rebuilding his personal power. To exalt the royal image he created a flamboyantly dazzling court and, more importantly, formed his own private standing army, for the traditional weakness of a feudal king was that he was forced to rely on his nobles to provide him with armed men.

Richard waited for eight years. Then, in 1397, he made his move. The three leading Lords Appellant were arrested. One was banished, one executed and one died in prison in suspicious circumstances. Parliament, understandably nervous, granted Richard powers greater than any English king had ever wielded before.

What is interesting to remember as the play begins is that the leader of the Lords Appellant, the one who was arrested by Richard and who died so mysteriously in prison, was Richard's own uncle, the Duke of Gloucester.

More interesting is the fact that the other two remaining Lords

Appellant who had taken part in Richard's humiliation in 1388 were Bullingbrook and Mowbray, now appearing before the king for judgement.

More interesting still is the fact that some historical sources claim that, shortly before he was arrested, Gloucester was plotting, together with Bullingbrook and Mowbray, another political coup. They planned to imprison Richard and his uncles, York and Lancaster, then put to death the rest of the King's Council. Mowbray, it is claimed, revealed this plot to Richard, who arrested Gloucester and had him sent to Calais.

What were Richard's intentions at the point where the play begins? Was he still out for revenge on the remaining two Lords Appellant who had so humiliated him? Or was Mowbray now a trusted supporter? If the king wished to be rid of Bullingbrook, he could not forget that Bullingbrook was not just a royal prince and cousin, but the son of Gaunt, Duke of Lancaster. Gaunt was the most powerful noble in England, chief counsellor and uncle to the king, almost as powerful as the king himself.

What might have been the thoughts of Bullingbrook and Mowbray as they entered for their trial? Their quarrel had apparently started when Bullingbrook accused Mowbray of treasonable talk, alleging in Parliament that Mowbray had confided to him his fears that Richard was now plotting to destroy the two of them as he had the other Lords Appellant.

Why should Bullingbrook have done this? Was it hatred of Mowbray or loyalty to the king? Was he indirectly attacking the king through one of his supporters, or was he trying to save his own skin by betraying Mowbray? Mowbray had naturally denied the charge and the whole affair was referred to the Court of Chivalry. Both men were put under arrest. Bullingbrook was released on bail under the charge of his father but Mowbray was detained in Windsor Castle. The two men must have feared for their lives.

Given King Richard's seemingly secure political position at the point where the play begins, his downfall is remarkably sudden. In April 1398 he was supremely powerful. In September 1399 he was forced to resign the throne in favour of Bullingbrook. By February 1400 he was dead.

How could it have happened so quickly? The play gives a fascinating view of an event that shook the Elizabethan world almost 200 years later.

As the play begins

A reconstruction of an Elizabethan stage.

This is what an Elizabethan audience might have seen as they settled to watch the opening of the play. The trumpeters in the gallery would play a 'flourish' to indicate that a royal personage was about to appear in a state procession.

Royal pageants and processions were a familiar sight to the Elizabethans. Many would have seen Elizabeth herself in royal progress. The actors would be magnificently dressed (quite literally so, for many of them purchased expensive costumes second-hand from the aristocracy for this very purpose). The stage itself, with its marble-painted pillars, impressive entrances and brightly coloured 'heavens' would very effectively suggest a royal court.

How would an Elizabethan audience have viewed Richard – as royal martyr or incompetent failure? What would they expect of Gaunt, the most powerful man in England after the king, or of his son, Bullingbrook, the future King Henry IV? It is not easy to be sure just how much historical knowledge an Elizabethan audience would have had. Some no doubt would merely enjoy the opening scene as a quarrel between two powerful men. Others would perhaps have had a very sophisticated awareness of the political manoeuvrings that lay behind the words.

And words there are in plenty in this very public and formal opening scene. It is not easy to decide exactly what is being thought and what people's true intentions are. You will have to study hard the silences that lie behind the words.

Get to know the opening scene (individually)

Before you look closely at Act 1 Scene 1, quickly read it through. Don't expect to understand everything at once. Try to get a sense of the kind of play you are reading and something of its special qualities. Certain kinds of understanding will only come when you actually speak and listen to the lines, or when you 'mentally put the play on the stage'.

Concentrate your attention in this read-through on the four speaking characters: King Richard, John of Gaunt, Henry Bullingbrook and Thomas Mowbray. Think about what they do, the way they speak and what they seem to think of each other.

Remember that you are in the Court of Chivalry, a special court of law formed to resolve disputes between men of high rank, and that around you are the most powerful men in the land, eager to witness the outcome of this trial.

List of characters

The Royal Family

KING RICHARD THE SECOND
QUEEN ISABEL King Richard's wife
JOHN OF GAUNT Duke of Lancaster (King Richard's uncle)
HENRY BULLINGBROOK Duke of Hereford; John of Gaunt's son;
    afterwards **King Henry IV**
DUKE OF YORK Edmund of Langley (King Richard's uncle)
DUCHESS OF YORK
DUKE OF AUMERLE Earl of Rutland, the Duke of York's son
DUCHESS OF GLOUCESTER widow of Thomas of Woodstock,
    Duke of Gloucester (King Richard's uncle)

Supporters of the King

THOMAS MOWBRAY Duke of Norfolk
SIR WILLIAM BAGOT king's minister and councillor
SIR JOHN BUSHY Speaker of the House of Commons
SIR HENRY GREEN councillor to the king
BISHOP OF CARLISLE
ABBOT OF WESTMINSTER
SIR STEPHEN SCROOPE

Supporters of Bullingbrook

EARL OF NORTHUMBERLAND   LORD ROSS
    Henry Percy   LORD WILLOUGHBY
HARRY PERCY (HOTSPUR) The   SIR PIERS OF EXTON
    Earl of Northumberland's son

The Court

EARL OF SALISBURY
LORD BERKELEY
LORD FITZWATER
DUKE OF SURREY
LORD MARSHAL
LADIES attending Queen Isabel

The People

CAPTAIN of the Welsh Army
GARDENER
TWO GARDENER'S MEN
KEEPER of the prison at Pomfret
SERVINGMAN
GROOM to King Richard

Attendant nobles, two heralds, soldiers, servants, murderers.

King Richard prepares to preside as judge over the quarrel between Henry Bullingbrook, Duke of Hereford, and Thomas Mowbray, Duke of Norfolk.

1 How do they speak to each other? (in groups of four)

Remember where you are in this opening scene and the kind of people who are around you. Take a character each and read this page out loud at least twice. If you can find space, try to stand several feet apart as you read. Talk about the way these men speak to each other and decide how impressive the king seems to be.

2 What does the king expect? (in pairs)

Take it in turns to read aloud lines 18–19 several times. As you listen to your partner, try to picture in your mind's eye what you hear. Then quickly write down or describe these images. Decide what Richard appears to think of the two men, Bullingbrook and Mowbray.

3 Royal king – powerful barons (in groups of six to eight)

Set out your stage area more or less as in the picture on page 3 and work out (or block) what you think are the basic stage moves for lines 1–29. Look for the 'internal stage directions' (the clues in the lines themselves – line 15 for example). The historical Richard demanded great shows of respect from his nobles with bowing, kneeling and kissing of hands, so make use of such pieces of stage business. Play it two ways:

- the barons show genuine fear and respect for Richard
- the barons are apparently respectful but under the surface are resentful, even insolent.

Which way seems more appropriate?

---

oath and band oath and bond
  (Gaunt was required to guarantee
  on oath that his son would appear
  to make good his accusations
  against Mowbray)
late appeal recent accusation

appeal the Duke accuses the duke
high stomached try walking
  around the room as if you were
  literally 'high stomached' and you
  will get the meaning!
ire anger

King Richard II

ACT I   SCENE I
The Throne Room

Enter KING RICHARD, JOHN OF GAUNT,
with other nobles and attendants

RICHARD Old John of Gaunt, time-honoured Lancaster,
  Hast thou according to thy oath and band
  Brought hither Henry Herford, thy bold son,
  Here to make good the boisterous late appeal,
  Which then our leisure would not let us hear,   5
  Against the Duke of Norfolk, Thomas Mowbray?
GAUNT I have, my liege.
RICHARD Tell me moreover hast thou sounded him
  If he appeal the Duke on ancient malice,
  Or worthily as a good subject should   10
  On some known ground of treachery in him?
GAUNT As near as I could sift him on that argument,
  On some apparent danger seen in him
  Aimed at your highness, no inveterate malice.
RICHARD Then call them to our presence. Face to face   15
  And frowning brow to brow ourselves will hear
  The accuser and the accusèd freely speak.
  High stomached are they both and full of ire,
  In rage deaf as the sea, hasty as fire.

   Enter BULLINGBROOK *and* MOWBRAY.

BULLINGBROOK Many years of happy days befall   20
  My gracious sovereign, my most loving liege.
MOWBRAY Each day still better other's happiness,
  Until the heavens, envying earth's good hap,
  Add an immortal title to your crown.
RICHARD We thank you both. Yet one but flatters us,   25
  As well appeareth by the cause you come,
  Namely to appeal each other of high treason.

Bullingbrook and Mowbray, accuser and accused, face each other.

---

1 Making an impression (in pairs)

In drama there is always a space around the speech and a specific purpose and target for the words. Stand up to do this activity (or do it sitting down if there is no room). Choose objects around you (chairs, tables, books) to represent the major characters present. Read the two speeches slowly and precisely, one of you as Bullingbrook, one as Mowbray. Point, gesture or move *clearly and deliberately* wherever you can. For example, lines 34–5:

'Come I [*point to yourself*] appellant to this princely presence' [*turn and point to King Richard*].
'Now Thomas Mowbray [*point to partner*] do I [*point to yourself*] turn [*do so*] to thee' [*point to partner*].

Talk about the impression you think these two men are trying to make on those around them.

2 Is this the language of a Court of Law?
(in groups of three to six)

If the Court of Chivalry could not resolve a dispute the inevitable consequence was for it to go to Trial by Combat.

Two of you slowly read this exchange, while the rest tap on the desk/table whenever a word or phrase strikes them powerfully (one or two words per line at most – perhaps none at all for some lines). Do it again, but this time the rest echo or repeat the words to create a more powerful effect. What kinds of words have you highlighted and what do they tell you of the feelings of these two men?

---

appellant making a formal accusation (Richard might well recall that here are the remaining two Lords Appellant who had so humiliated him in 1388)
miscreant literally 'unbeliever' (hence a general term of abuse)

aggravate the note emphasise the disgrace
right drawn justly drawn
arbitrate decide
post ride swiftly

     Cousin of Herford, what dost thou object
     Against the Duke of Norfolk, Thomas Mowbray?
BULLINGBROOK First, heaven be the record to my speech.   30
     In the devotion of a subject's love,
     Tendering the precious safety of my prince,
     And free from other misbegotten hate,
     Come I appellant to this princely presence.
     Now Thomas Mowbray do I turn to thee,   35
     And mark my greeting well; for what I speak
     My body shall make good upon this earth,
     Or my divine soul answer it in heaven.
     Thou art a traitor and a miscreant,
     Too good to be so, and too bad to live.   40
     Since the more fair and crystal is the sky,
     The uglier seem the clouds that in it fly.
     Once more, the more to aggravate the note,
     With a foul traitor's name stuff I thy throat,
     And wish (so please my sovereign) ere I move,   45
     What my tongue speaks my right drawn sword may prove.
MOWBRAY Let not my cold words here accuse my zeal.
     'Tis not the trial of a woman's war,
     The bitter clamour of two eager tongues,
     Can arbitrate this cause betwixt us twain.   50
     The blood is hot that must be cooled for this.
     Yet can I not of such tame patience boast
     As to be hushed, and naught at all to say.
     First, the fair reverence of your highness curbs me
     From giving reins and spurs to my free speech,   55
     Which else would post until it had returned
     These terms of treason doubled down his throat.
     Setting aside his high blood's royalty,
     And let him be no kinsman to my liege,
     I do defy him, and I spit at him,   60
     Call him a slanderous coward and a villain,
     Which to maintain I would allow him odds
     And meet him were I tied to run afoot
     Even to the frozen ridges of the Alps,
     Or any other ground inhabitable   65
     Where ever Englishman durst set his foot.
     Meantime, let this defend my loyalty:
     By all my hopes most falsely doth he lie.

Bullingbrook challenges Mowbray to Trial by Combat and is promptly accepted. Richard demands of Bullingbrook the reasons for his challenge.

---

1 What accusations does Bullingbrook make?
(in groups of threes)

Read lines 87–108 taking a sentence each. Listen to the crimes that Bullingbrook accuses Mowbray of committing. Make a list of them and decide which alleged crimes are the most serious or most likely to have been committed by Mowbray. It may help you to know that Mowbray was about thirty-two years old at this time. He was Governor of Calais where Gloucester mysteriously died.

2 'Streams of blood' (in small groups)

Look at lines 98–106 and think about the biblical story of Cain and Abel (Genesis 4 v.3–12). Why might some of those watching this trial think that Bullingbrook is after bigger fish than Mowbray?

Look back over the play so far and find any other lines that refer to 'blood'. In what different senses is it used? Be alert to this word – you will hear it many more times!

3 Stage picture

The pattern or grouping that is set up in this opening scene is symbolically very important. You will find it echoed in many ways in later scenes, so get your own conception of it clear.

Read lines 69–83 and draw a sketch of how you think the characters should be placed on stage at the moment indicated by line 78. Use the illustration of an Elizabethan stage on page 3, or design your own stage set if you wish. Include all the major characters plus other figures (trumpeters, attendants, nobles, bishops).

---

gage glove
makes thee to except prompts you
  to set aside
inherit us make us think
look what whatever

nobles coins
lendings advances on pay
lewd employments improper use
suggest prompted or incited

BULLINGBROOK Pale trembling coward, there I throw my gage,
    Disclaiming here the kindred of the king, 70
    And lay aside my high blood's royalty,
    Which fear, not reverence, makes thee to except.
    If guilty dread have left thee so much strength
    As to take up mine honour's pawn, then stoop.
    By that and all the rites of knighthood else 75
    Will I make good against thee, arm to arm,
    What I have spoke, or thou canst worse devise.
MOWBRAY I take it up, and by that sword I swear
    Which gently laid my knighthood on my shoulder
    I'll answer thee in any fair degree 80
    Or chivalrous design of knightly trial;
    And when I mount, alive may I not light
    If I be traitor or unjustly fight.
RICHARD What doth our cousin lay to Mowbray's charge?
    It must be great that can inherit us 85
    So much as of a thought of ill in him.
BULLINGBROOK Look what I speak, my life shall prove it true:
    That Mowbray hath received eight thousand nobles
    In name of lendings for your highness' soldiers,
    The which he hath detained for lewd employments 90
    Like a false traitor and injurious villain.
    Besides I say, and will in battle prove
    Or here or elsewhere to the furthest verge
    That ever was surveyed by English eye,
    That all the treasons for these eighteen years 95
    Complotted and contrivèd in this land
    Fetch from false Mowbray their first head and spring.
    Further I say, and further will maintain
    Upon his bad life to make all this good,
    That he did plot the Duke of Gloucester's death, 100
    Suggest his soon-believing adversaries,
    And consequently like a traitor coward
    Sluiced out his innocent soul through streams of blood,
    Which blood, like sacrificing Abel's, cries
    Even from the tongueless caverns of the earth 105
    To me for justice and rough chastisement;
    And, by the glorious worth of my descent,
    This arm shall do it, or this life be spent.

Richard gives Mowbray leave to make his defence.

1 Can Mowbray trust King Richard? (in pairs)

Will Richard truly be impartial? Bullingbrook is after all cousin to the king and a powerful prince. First remind yourselves of the background to this quarrel (pages 1–2). Then sit face to face. Take a part each and speak lines 111–25 to each other. At the end of each line of the king's words, Mowbray must comment out loud on what the king is saying. Exchange roles and try it again. Then perhaps try it with Richard sounding very genuine or very insincere. Decide if you can be sure of the king's true feelings here.

2 Is Mowbray telling the truth? (in groups of four)

Each person takes a sentence in turn and reads Mowbray's defence speech (lines 124–49). Then one of the group reads the whole speech while the others close their eyes and listen to the way Mowbray puts his thoughts and sentences together. Decide how well he defends himself.

Now study the details of the speech very closely in the manner of a political commentator. Get clear in your minds the four or five points that Mowbray makes in answer to Bullingbrook's accusations. What do you believe and what do you find suspicious?

What does Mowbray's comment concerning the Duke of Lancaster suggest is the general standard of political morality at this time?

---

pitch height a falcon flies before attacking (a falcon was also one of Bullingbrook's emblems)
slander of his blood disgrace to the royal blood (i.e. Bullingbrook)
receipt . . . Calais money given to pay the garrison at Calais
ere before

sacrament Christian ritual of Holy Communion
confess i.e. confessed his sins to the priest
rancour bitterness, spite
recreant coward
interchangeably in return

RICHARD How high a pitch his resolution soars!
      Thomas of Norfolk, what say'st thou to this?   110
MOWBRAY Oh let my sovereign turn away his face
      And bid his ears a little while be deaf,
      Till I have told this slander of his blood
      How God and good men hate so foul a liar.
RICHARD Mowbray, impartial are our eyes and ears.   115
      Were he my brother, nay, my kingdom's heir,
      As he is but my father's brother's son,
      Now by my sceptre's awe I make a vow
      Such neighbour nearness to our sacred blood
      Should nothing privilege him nor partialise   120
      The unstooping firmness of my upright soul.
      He is our subject, Mowbray; so art thou.
      Free speech and fearless I to thee allow.
MOWBRAY Then, Bullingbrook, as low as to thy heart
      Through the false passage of thy throat thou liest.   125
      Three parts of that receipt I had for Calais
      Disbursed I duly to his highness' soldiers.
      The other part reserved I by consent,
      For that my sovereign liege was in my debt
      Upon remainder of a dear account   130
      Since last I went to France to fetch his queen.
      Now swallow down that lie. For Gloucester's death,
      I slew him not, but to my own disgrace
      Neglected my sworn duty in that case.
      For you, my noble lord of Lancaster,   135
      The honourable father to my foe,
      Once did I lay an ambush for your life,
      A trespass that doth vex my grievèd soul.
      But ere I last received the sacrament
      I did confess it, and exactly begged   140
      Your grace's pardon, and I hope I had it.
      This is my fault. As for the rest appealed,
      It issues from the rancour of a villain,
      A recreant and most degenerate traitor,
      Which in myself I boldly will defend,   145
      And interchangeably hurl down my gage
      Upon this overweening traitor's foot,

*Richard attempts a reconciliation between the two feuding lords
but neither man will yield.*

---

1 Richard the peacemaker (in groups of four)

When you are reading a script it is very easy to forget that characters
who may be silent at that moment are in fact very powerfully present.
The 1980 RSC production records the following moves and positions
for lines 150–76:

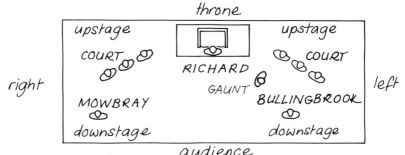

a Start of line 150: Mowbray (M) throws down gage and kneels.
   Bullingbrook (B) moves towards him and King (K) moves to
   between them.

b Start of line 158: K moves to right of Gaunt (G). M stands.

c End of line 159: K moves to left of M. G moves a step downstage.

d Start of line 161: B picks up M's gage and returns Down Centre
   Left.

e Middle of line 162: G moves Up Right of B.

f Start of line 165: M kneels.

g Start of line 175: M stands.

Find a large space in the hall or drama studio and try these moves for
yourselves. What picture do you create of the four men?

---

choler anger (choler and blood
  were two of the humours – see page
  200)
no month to bleed doctors used
  astrology to decide on the right
  times for treating (i.e. bleeding)
  their patients

impeached accused in law
baffled publicly dishonoured for
  cowardice
lions . . . leopards Mowbray's coat
  of arms contained a leopard

                   To prove myself a loyal gentleman
                   Even in the best blood chambered in his bosom.
                   In haste whereof most heartily I pray   150
                   Your highness to assign our trial day.
RICHARD Wrath-kindled gentlemen, be ruled by me.
                   Let's purge this choler without letting blood.
                   This we prescribe though no physician.
                   Deep malice makes too deep incision.   155
                   Forget, forgive, conclude and be agreed.
                   Our doctors say this is no month to bleed.
                   Good uncle, let this end where it begun,
                   We'll calm the Duke of Norfolk, you your son.
GAUNT To be a make-peace shall become my age.   160
                   Throw down, my son, the Duke of Norfolk's gage.
RICHARD And, Norfolk, throw down his.
GAUNT   When, Harry, when?
                   Obedience bids I should not bid again.
RICHARD Norfolk, throw down we bid; there is no boot.
MOWBRAY Myself I throw, dread sovereign, at thy foot.   165
                   My life thou shalt command, but not my shame.
                   The one my duty owes, but my fair name,
                   Despite of death, that lives upon my grave,
                   To dark dishonour's use thou shalt not have.
                   I am disgraced, impeached and baffled here,   170
                   Pierced to the soul with slander's venomed spear,
                   The which no balm can cure but his heart blood
                   Which breathed this poison.
RICHARD   Rage must be withstood.
                   Give me his gage. Lions make leopards tame.
MOWBRAY Yea, but not change his spots. Take but my shame   175
                   And I resign my gage. My dear, dear lord,
                   The purest treasure mortal times afford
                   Is spotless reputation; that away,
                   Men are but gilded loam, or painted clay.
                   A jewel in a ten times barred up chest   180
                   Is a bold spirit in a loyal breast.
                   Mine honour is my life, both grow in one.
                   Take honour from me and my life is done.
                   Then, dear my liege, mine honour let me try.
                   In that I live, and for that will I die.   185

Since both lords refuse to be reconciled, Richard accepts their desire to fight.
He appoints the day and place for the Trial by Combat.

---

1 What is your picture of King Richard? (in small groups)

Remind yourselves of the fifty-seven lines Richard speaks in this scene. Decide which of these pictures best fits your idea of him. Justify your choice by reference to Richard's words and actions.

| Ian McKellen as King Richard. | Portrait of the real King Richard. | John Gielgud as King Richard. |

2 The real battle? (in pairs)

For the first time, Richard gives a direct command to Bullingbrook. Speak lines 186–205 to each other, one as Richard, one as Bullingbrook. Who comes out the winner?

---

impeach my height disgrace my high rank
dastard coward
parle trumpet call for a truce
motive tongue (literally a moving limb)

his high disgrace his tongue's
sue beg
atone reconcile
justice . . . chivalry God's justice ensure that the right man wins

RICHARD Cousin, throw up your gage. Do you begin.
BULLINGBROOK O God defend my soul from such deep sin!
        Shall I seem crestfallen in my father's sight?
        Or with pale beggar fear impeach my height
        Before this out-dared dastard? Ere my tongue   190
        Shall wound my honour with such feeble wrong,
        Or sound so base a parle, my teeth shall tear
        The slavish motive of recanting fear
        And spit it bleeding in his high disgrace,
        Where shame doth harbour, even in Mowbray's face.   195

                                   Exit Gaunt

RICHARD We were not born to sue, but to command,
        Which, since we cannot do to make you friends,
        Be ready, as your lives shall answer it,
        At Coventry upon Saint Lambert's Day.
        There shall your swords and lances arbitrate   200
        The swelling difference of your settled hate.
        Since we cannot atone you, we shall see
        Justice design the victor's chivalry.
        Lord Marshal, command our officers at arms
        Be ready to direct these home alarms.   205

                                   Exeunt

The Duchess of Gloucester attempts to incite John of Gaunt to avenge the murder of his brother, the Duke of Gloucester.

---

1 Who killed the Duke of Gloucester? (in pairs)

The ghost of the Duke of Gloucester haunts this play. Take a part each and read this scene straight through. Does what Gaunt and the duchess say concerning the murder change your attitude to the events in the opening scene?

2 Picture the deed (in groups of four)

Turn to page 193 and study the picture of a medieval Tree of Jesse. Talk about what connections it seems to have with this play.

Have paper and a pencil/pen ready. As one person slowly reads lines 11–21, the rest close their eyes and picture what is being expressed. Do this at least twice then quickly draw the picture you have in your mind. Look at your different versions. What kind of world does the duchess believe she is in?

---

part . . . blood 'blood' here implies kinship (not murder)

since . . . correct only the king can punish, but it is the king himself who is guilty

Edward's seven sons (see page 192 for genealogical tree)

vials small glass bottles, phials

self same

model copy, image

mean ordinary, common

venge avenge

18

ACT 1 SCENE 2
John of Gaunt's house

Enter JOHN OF GAUNT with the DUCHESS OF GLOUCESTER

GAUNT Alas, the part I had in Woodstock's blood
    Doth more solicit me than your exclaims
    To stir against the butchers of his life.
    But since correction lieth in those hands
    Which made the fault that we cannot correct,   5
    Put we our quarrel to the will of heaven,
    Who when they see the hours ripe on earth
    Will rain hot vengeance on offenders' heads.
DUCHESS Finds brotherhood in thee no sharper spur?
    Hath love in thy old blood no living fire?   10
    Edward's seven sons, whereof thyself art one,
    Were as seven vials of his sacred blood,
    Or seven fair branches springing from one root.
    Some of those seven are dried by nature's course,
    Some of those branches by the Destinies cut,   15
    But Thomas, my dear lord, my life, my Gloucester,
    One vial full of Edward's sacred blood,
    One flourishing branch of his most royal root,
    Is cracked, and all the precious liquor spilt,
    Is hacked down, and his summer leaves all faded,   20
    By envy's hand, and murder's bloody axe.
    Ah, Gaunt, his blood was thine; that bed, that womb,
    That mettle, that self mould, that fashioned thee
    Made him a man; and though thou liv'st and breath'st
    Yet art thou slain in him. Thou dost consent   25
    In some large measure to thy father's death
    In that thou seest thy wretched brother die,
    Who was the model of thy father's life.
    Call it not patience, Gaunt. It is despair.
    In suffering thus thy brother to be slaughtered   30
    Thou showest the naked pathway to thy life,
    Teaching stern murder how to butcher thee.
    That which in mean men we entitle patience
    Is pale cold cowardice in noble breasts.

Gaunt feels unable to gain revenge for Gloucester's murder because he believes that it was the king himself who ordered it. Only God can avenge a crime committed by his anointed deputy.

1 What mood is the duchess in? (any size of group)

Try 'walking the line' to help you with this. Read lines 58–74 to yourself. Next walk around the hall/studio while you read these lines aloud, but remember to pause in your reading and turn ninety degrees whenever you come to a punctuation mark. Although the punctuation marks are not Shakespeare's but a later addition, they will reflect the thought structures, so your movements will physically match the patterns and rhythms of the sentence. Talk about what your walking tells you of the duchess's moods and feelings here.

2 The truth behind the splendour (in small groups)

This scene, unlike the opening scene and the one which follows, is not based on any historical record and seems to be entirely Shakespeare's invention. Talk about why you think Shakespeare included it.

3 What is the duchess like?

This is the only time we see the Duchess of Gloucester. Does your impression of her in any way resemble the woman in this drawing?

God's substitute . . . deputy
  anointed see pages 198–9 for
  details of late medieval and
  Elizabethan beliefs concerning the
  nature of kingship
fell fierce, cruel

career charge or encounter
courser horse
lists enclosed area where the
  combatants would fight
caitiff recreant captive coward

What shall I say? To safeguard thine own life   35
The best way is to venge my Gloucester's death.
GAUNT God's is the quarrel, for God's substitute,
His deputy anointed in His sight,
Hath caused his death, the which if wrongfully
Let heaven revenge, for I may never lift   40
An angry arm against His minister.
DUCHESS Where then, alas, may I complain myself?
GAUNT To God, the widow's champion and defence.
DUCHESS Why then I will. Farewell, old Gaunt.
Thou goest to Coventry, there to behold   45
Our cousin Herford and fell Mowbray fight.
Oh, set my husband's wrongs on Herford's spear,
That it may enter butcher Mowbray's breast!
Or if misfortune miss the first career
Be Mowbray's sins so heavy in his bosom   50
That they may break his foaming courser's back,
And throw the rider headlong in the lists,
A caitiff recreant to my cousin Herford.
Farewell, old Gaunt. Thy sometime brother's wife
With her companion grief must end her life.   55
GAUNT Sister, farewell. I must to Coventry.
As much good stay with thee as go with me.
DUCHESS Yet one word more. Grief boundeth where it falls,
Not with the empty hollowness, but weight.
I take my leave before I have begun,   60
For sorrow ends not when it seemeth done.
Commend me to thy brother Edmund York.
Lo, this is all. Nay, yet depart not so;
Though this be all, do not so quickly go.
I shall remember more. Bid him, ah, what?   65
With all good speed at Plashy visit me.
Alack, and what shall good old York there see
But empty lodgings and unfurnished walls,
Unpeopled offices, untrodden stones,
And what hear there for welcome but my groans?   70
Therefore commend me, let him not come there,
To seek out sorrow that dwells everywhere.
Desolate, desolate will I hence and die.
The last leave of thee takes my weeping eye.
                                                    Exeunt

Richard and his nobles prepare to witness the Trial by Combat between Bullingbrook and Mowbray.

1 Pageantry or brutality? (in groups of three)

The Trial by Combat between Bullingbrook and Mowbray was a dazzlingly magnificent event. Two of England's most famous knights were to fight before the assembled Chivalry of England.

For the actual combatants the day was to be more savage. The loser, if still alive, would be dragged from the lists (the enclosed combat area), to a place of execution to be hanged or beheaded.

Take a part each and read lines 7–25. Stand some distance apart. Does the language highlight the pageantry or the brutality of the occasion?

---

at all points completely
appellant accuser
God defend God forbid

truth honesty, integrity, loyalty, nobility – in fact all the qualities of a true knight (the historical Mowbray fell rather short of this ideal)
appeals accuses

ACT 1   SCENE 3
The lists at Coventry

Enter Lord MARSHAL *and the Duke* AUMERLE

MARSHAL My Lord Aumerle, is Harry Herford armed?
AUMERLE Yea, at all points, and longs to enter in.
MARSHAL The Duke of Norfolk, sprightfully and bold,
  Stays but the summons of the appellant's trumpet.
AUMERLE Why then, the champions are prepared and stay   5
  For nothing but his majesty's approach.

The trumpets sound and the King RICHARD *enters with his nobles; when they are
set, enter* MOWBRAY *the Duke of Norfolk in arms defendant.*

RICHARD Marshal, demand of yonder champion
  The cause of his arrival here in arms.
  Ask him his name, and orderly proceed
  To swear him in the justice of his cause.   10
MARSHAL In God's name and the king's say who thou art,
  And why thou com'st thus knightly clad in arms,
  Against what man thou comest and what thy quarrel.
  Speak truly on thy knighthood and thy oath,
  And so defend thee heaven and thy valour.   15
MOWBRAY My name is Thomas Mowbray, Duke of Norfolk,
  Who hither come engagèd by my oath
  (Which God defend a knight should violate)
  Both to defend my loyalty and truth
  To God, my king, and my succeeding issue,   20
  Against the Duke of Herford that appeals me,
  And by the grace of God, and this mine arm,
  To prove him, in defending of myself,
  A traitor to my God, my king, and me.
  And as I truly fight, defend me heaven.   25

Bullingbrook takes leave of his king.

1 Ritual (in groups of five or more)

The whole process of Trial by Combat was regarded as archaic even in Richard II's time. Like us, an Elizabethan audience must have found it rather strange.

Identify the different characters in the picture and then present a version to the class of lines 1–45 and 99–117 which has a similarly ceremonial atmosphere. Remember that God was supposed to decide the outcome of a Trial by Combat. The Bishop of Carlisle is on the cast list. Can you make use of him in your presentation?

plated in habiliments of war wearing plate armour

depose him ask him to state his case under oath

pilgrimage this image will become very significant to Bullingbrook by the end of the play

lament . . . dead I'll grieve for you, but take no further action (defeat proved a man's guilt in Trial by Combat)

falcon Bullingbrook's emblem

The trumpets sound. Enter BULLINGBROOK Duke of Herford
appellant in armour

RICHARD Marshal, demand of yonder knight in arms
    Both who he is and why he cometh hither
    Thus plated in habiliments of war,
    And formally according to our law
    Depose him in the justice of his cause.   30
MARSHAL What is thy name? And wherefore com'st thou hither
    Before King Richard in his royal lists?
    Against whom comest thou, and what's thy quarrel?
    Speak like a true knight, so defend thee heaven.
BULLINGBROOK Harry of Herford, Lancaster and Derby 35
    Am I, who ready here do stand in arms
    To prove by God's grace and my body's valour
    In lists, on Thomas Mowbray, Duke of Norfolk,
    That he's a traitor foul and dangerous
    To God of heaven, King Richard and to me; 40
    And as I truly fight, defend me heaven.
MARSHAL On pain of death, no person be so bold
    Or daring-hardy as to touch the lists,
    Except the Marshal and such officers
    Appointed to direct these fair designs.   45
BULLINGBROOK Lord Marshal, let me kiss my sovereign's hand
    And bow my knee before his majesty,
    For Mowbray and myself are like two men
    That vow a long and weary pilgrimage.
    Then let us take a ceremonious leave 50
    And loving farewell of our several friends.
MARSHAL The appellant in all duty greets your highness,
    And craves to kiss your hand and take his leave.
RICHARD We will descend and fold him in our arms.
    Cousin of Herford, as thy cause is right 55
    So be thy fortune in this royal fight.
    Farewell, my blood, which if today thou shed
    Lament we may, but not revenge the dead.
BULLINGBROOK Oh, let no noble eye profane a tear
    For me, if I be gored with Mowbray's spear. 60
    As confident as is the falcon's flight
    Against a bird do I with Mowbray fight.

Both combatants take their leave of the assembled company.

---

1 Going to their death (in groups of four)

There was much ceremony in Elizabethan life. Leave-taking required embraces, hand-clasps, kisses and other gestures. Try the following activities:

a Richard's farewell to Bullingbrook (lines 46–58)
Show how you think the king takes leave of his cousin.
b Bullingbrook's farewells (lines 59–84)
Show how he takes leave of Richard, Aumerle and Gaunt.
c Mowbray's farewells (lines 85–99)
Make this leave-taking different to Bullingbrook's.

When you have tried all three, put them together into a mime or dumb show and present it to the rest of the class.

2 Where do Richard's sympathies lie? (in pairs)

Take it in turns to read Richard's farewell words to the two men (lines 54–8 and lines 97–9). Can you decide which man the king favours?

---

regreet the daintiest last welcome last of all the sweetest tasting dish (even in those days the English finished their meals with a sweet dessert!)
regenerate re-born
lusty strong, vigorous
haviour behaviour

casque helmet
enfranchisement release from imprisonment
jocund happy
jest sport, game
couchèd levelled in readiness (as a lance)

My loving lord, I take my leave of you.
Of you, my noble cousin, Lord Aumerle,
Not sick, although I have to do with death,   65
But lusty, young and cheerly drawing breath.
Lo, as at English feasts so I regreet
The daintiest last, to make the end most sweet.
Oh thou, the earthly author of my blood,
Whose youthful spirit in me regenerate   70
Doth with a twofold vigour lift me up
To reach at victory above my head,
Add proof unto mine armour with thy prayers,
And with thy blessings steel my lance's point
That it may enter Mowbray's waxen coat,   75
And furbish new the name of John a Gaunt
Even in the lusty haviour of his son.
GAUNT God in thy good cause make thee prosperous.
Be swift like lightning in the execution
And let thy blows, doubly redoubled,   80
Fall like amazing thunder on the casque
Of thy adverse pernicious enemy.
Rouse up thy youthful blood, be valiant and live.
BULLINGBROOK Mine innocency and Saint George to thrive.
MOWBRAY However God or Fortune cast my lot   85
There lives or dies, true to King Richard's throne,
A loyal, just and upright gentleman.
Never did captive with a freer heart
Cast off his chains of bondage and embrace
His golden uncontrolled enfranchisement   90
More than my dancing soul doth celebrate
This feast of battle with mine adversary.
Most mighty liege and my companion peers,
Take from my mouth the wish of happy years.
As gentle and as jocund as to jest   95
Go I to fight. Truth hath a quiet breast.
RICHARD Farewell, my lord. Securely I espy
Virtue with valour couchèd in thine eye.
Order the trial, Marshal, and begin.

The signal is given for the combat to begin but at the last moment Richard stops the proceedings.

---

1 Tension and shock (in groups of eight)

The Chronicles record how the king's intervention at the last moment created a veritable sensation.

Present a snapshot photograph (a 'tableau' or 'frozen moment') showing the effect of the king's action (line 118). It may help you to create the tableau if you decide on the movements and gestures for lines 100–18, walk them through, then freeze at line 118 in your different positions and gestures. Be imaginative. One production had two nobles leaping over the barriers of the lists to separate the fighters.

Take time to rehearse this. Then show your snapshot to the other groups. Hold the freeze position for about thirty seconds so that the others can identify exactly who is who.

---

recreant cowardly
approve prove
warder ceremonial baton (throwing it down signalled the instant ending of the fight)
while we return until we inform

flourish a fanfare of trumpets to announce the arrival or departure of a monarch. What does that tell you of Richard's movements in lines 121–4?
list hear, listen to

MARSHAL Harry of Herford, Lancaster and Derby, 100
     Receive thy lance, and God defend the right.
BULLINGBROOK Strong as a tower in hope, I cry amen.
MARSHAL Go bear this lance to Thomas Duke of Norfolk.
1 HERALD Harry of Herford, Lancaster and Derby
     Stands here, for God, his sovereign and himself, 105
     On pain to be found false and recreant,
     To prove the Duke of Norfolk, Thomas Mowbray,
     A traitor to his God, his king, and him,
     And dares him to set forward to the fight.
2 HERALD Here standeth Thomas Mowbray, Duke of Norfolk, 110
     On pain to be found false and recreant,
     Both to defend himself, and to approve
     Henry of Herford, Lancaster and Derby
     To God, his sovereign, and to him disloyal,
     Courageously and with a free desire, 115
     Attending but the signal to begin.
MARSHAL Sound trumpets, and set forward combatants.
               A charge sounded.

     Stay, the king hath thrown his warder down.
RICHARD Let them lay by their helmets and their spears,
     And both return back to their chairs again. 120
     Withdraw with us, and let the trumpets sound
     While we return these dukes what we decree.
               A long flourish.
     Draw near,
     And list what with our Council we have done.

*Richard sentences both men to exile – Bullingbrook for ten years,
Mowbray for life.*

---

1 What happened at the King's Council? (in groups of six)

The actual meeting lasted for two hours while the combatants
festered in their tents. It was probably a very stormy session and
Shakespeare must have been very tempted to include it. Sit around a
table and improvise the scene in the Council meeting. Those present:
Richard, Gaunt, Aumerle and other nobles supporting either Bullingbrook or Mowbray. Take time to prepare this meeting and try, as
the politicians say, to bring about a 'frank exchange of views'. What
do you think happened at the meeting to cause Mowbray to be
banished for life while Bullingbrook only gets ten years?

2 A crucial decision

The king was perfectly within his rights to halt a Trial by Combat, but
why on earth did he do so? If the combat had gone ahead and
Mowbray had killed Bullingbrook, the whole course of English
history might have changed and Richard might not have lost his
crown.

Richard's publicly-stated reason for halting the combat (lines
125–39) seems to be that he wished to preserve peace in the land. But
what other reasons might he have had?

---

for that in order that
and for and because
dire aspect awful appearance
set on you incited you
stranger foreign

doom judgement
determinate bring to an end
cunning skilfully made, or needing
  skill to play

For that our kingdom's earth should not be soiled   125
With that dear blood which it hath fosterèd,
And for our eyes do hate the dire aspect
Of civil wounds ploughed up with neighbour's sword,
And for we think the eagle-wingèd pride
Of sky-aspiring and ambitious thoughts   130
With rival-hating envy set on you
To wake our peace, which in our country's cradle
Draws the sweet infant breath of gentle sleep,
Which so roused up with boisterous untuned drums,
With harsh resounding trumpet's dreadful bray   135
And grating shock of wrathful iron arms,
Might from our quiet confines fright fair peace,
And make us wade even in our kindred's blood,
Therefore we banish you our territories.
You, cousin Herford, upon pain of life,   140
Till twice five summers have enriched our fields
Shall not regreet our fair dominions,
But tread the stranger paths of banishment.
BULLINGBROOK Your will be done. This must my comfort be:
That sun that warms you here shall shine on me,   145
And those his golden beams to you here lent
Shall point on me and gild my banishment.
RICHARD Norfolk, for thee remains a heavier doom,
Which I with some unwillingness pronounce.
The sly slow hours shall not determinate   150
The dateless limit of thy dear exile.
The hopeless word of never to return
Breathe I against thee, upon pain of life.
MOWBRAY A heavy sentence, my most sovereign liege,
And all unlooked for from your highness' mouth.   155
A dearer merit, not so deep a maim
As to be cast forth in the common air,
Have I deservèd at your highness' hands.
The language I have learnt these forty years,
My native English, now I must forgo,   160
And now my tongue's use is to me no more
Than an unstringèd viol or a harp,
Or like a cunning instrument cased up,

Before Mowbray departs into exile, Richard requires both men to swear an oath that they will never conspire against him.

---

1 Fill the silences behind the words (in groups of six)

What are Richard, Bullingbrook and Mowbray thinking as they perform the ritual of swearing the oath?

Three of you take one part each and read lines 170–91 while the others consider what the outer words might reveal (or conceal) about the inner thoughts of these three men.

Now dramatise your ideas by creating *alter egos* (or dual personalities). Three readers speak the lines slowly while the others become their *alter egos*, interrupting at certain points to speak that character's secret thoughts. You could perhaps have one *alter ego* speaking from behind or beside each character. Work this through several times until you are happy with it, then present your version to the rest of the class.

2 What must Bullingbrook and Mowbray never do? (in groups of five)

Two pairs stand face to face. The fifth student slowly reads Richard's orders (lines 178–90). You must mime with your partner all the things that you are told you must not do. You may find this enjoyable and revealing!

3 Silent pictures (in groups of three)

Read lines 119–211 and devise a silent movie version of this sad moment. Make it as sentimental as you can. One good way to prepare this is to write down all the movements and emotions in order, then put the script to one side and just work from the notes. Do you think it is effective to play it this way?

---

portcullised barred
it boots . . . compassionate it is
  pointless to demand sympathy
plaining complaining
take an oath the historical Richard
  made great use of oaths to enforce
  loyalty to the crown

louring frowning
complot plot together
sepulchre tomb
burthen burden

Or being open, put into his hands
That knows no touch to tune the harmony.   165
Within my mouth you have engaoled my tongue,
Doubly portcullised with my teeth and lips,
And dull unfeeling barren ignorance
Is made my gaoler to attend on me.
I am too old to fawn upon a nurse,   170
Too far in years to be a pupil now.
What is thy sentence then but speechless death,
Which robs my tongue from breathing native breath?

RICHARD It boots thee not to be compassionate.
        After our sentence plaining comes too late.   175

MOWBRAY Then thus I turn me from my country's light
        To dwell in solemn shades of endless night.

RICHARD Return again, and take an oath with thee.
        Lay on our royal sword your banished hands.
        Swear by the duty that you owe to God   180
        (Our part therein we banish with yourselves)
        To keep the oath that we administer.
        You never shall, so help you truth and God,
        Embrace each other's love in banishment,
        Nor never look upon each other's face,   185
        Nor never write, regreet nor reconcile
        This louring tempest of your home-bred hate,
        Nor never by advisèd purpose meet
        To plot, contrive or complot any ill
        'Gainst us, our state, our subjects or our land.   190

BULLINGBROOK I swear.

MOWBRAY   And I, to keep all this.

BULLINGBROOK Norfolk, so far as to mine enemy:
        By this time, had the king permitted us,
        One of our souls had wandered in the air,
        Banished this frail sepulchre of our flesh,   195
        As now our flesh is banished from this land.
        Confess thy treasons ere thou fly the realm.
        Since thou hast far to go, bear not along
        The clogging burthen of a guilty soul.

*After Mowbray's departure, Richard reduces Bullingbrook's term of
banishment from ten to six years.*

---

1 'We know what Heaven or Hell may bring, But no man knoweth the mind of the king.'

(in groups of four)   Rudyard Kipling

Some chroniclers state that Richard became increasingly tyrannical in
the last years of his reign. Yet they also record that he arrived for the
Combat with 20,000 archers and men-at-arms, which suggests that
he did not feel entirely secure.

Take a character each and read lines 200–47 (to where Richard
leaves). Talk about what you think is in the mind of the king and why
he should now reduce Bullingbrook's term of banishment. How
confident does he seem to be?

2 Flickering emotions (in pairs)

Take it in turns to read the following: lines 203–04, lines 207–08, line
212, lines 215–16, lines 222–3, line 224, line 225, line 232. Pause
after each one. Your partner must say what that speaker is really
thinking. Share your impressions with other pairs.

3 'And blindfold Death not let me see my son' (in groups of three to five)

Construct a tableau (or frozen moment) to illustrate line 223. Show
your version to the rest of the class.

---

rue regret
wanton luxuriant
current with him valid with time

thy tongue a party verdict gave it
was a joint decision which you
agreed to
lour frown, scowl

MOWBRAY No, Bullingbrook. If ever I were traitor,   200
        My name be blotted from the book of life
        And I from heaven banished as from hence.
        But what thou art, God, thou and I do know,
        And all too soon, I fear, the king shall rue.
        Farewell, my liege. Now no way can I stray.   205
        Save back to England all the world's my way.   *Exit*
RICHARD Uncle, even in the glasses of thine eyes
        I see thy grievèd heart. Thy sad aspect
        Hath from the number of his banished years
        Plucked four away. [*To Bullingbrook*] Six frozen winters
            spent,   210
        Return with welcome home from banishment.
BULLINGBROOK How long a time lies in one little word.
        Four lagging winters and four wanton springs
        End in a word, such is the breath of kings.
GAUNT I thank my liege that in regard of me   215
        He shortens four years of my son's exile;
        But little vantage shall I reap thereby,
        For ere the six years that he hath to spend
        Can change their moons and bring their times about
        My oil-dried lamp and time-bewasted light   220
        Shall be extinct with age and endless night,
        My inch of taper will be burnt and done,
        And blindfold Death not let me see my son.
RICHARD Why uncle, thou hast many years to live.
GAUNT But not a minute, king, that thou canst give.   225
        Shorten my days thou canst with sullen sorrow,
        And pluck nights from me, but not lend a morrow.
        Thou canst help time to furrow me with age,
        But stop no wrinkle in his pilgrimage.
        Thy word is current with him for my death,   230
        But dead thy kingdom cannot buy my breath.
RICHARD Thy son is banished upon good advice,
        Whereto thy tongue a party verdict gave.
        Why at our justice seemst thou then to lour?

Richard takes his leave of Bullingbrook and departs with his court.
Bullingbrook is left to bid his father farewell.

---

1 Father and son (in pairs)

For all his speeches in the opening scenes, Bullingbrook is silent on many things. What must he think of a father who has agreed to his own son's banishment?

Rehearse lines 252–73 in different ways, one as Gaunt, one as Bullingbrook (perhaps reading the lines face to face, or with Bullingbrook walking or turning away so that Gaunt has to follow). How frank and open are they towards each other?

2 What's Gaunt like?

'Gaunt lay like a dark shadow over the land', 'arrogant, flamboyant and boastful . . . he behaved for all the world as if he were already a monarch.' Compare these judgements made by some historians about the historical Gaunt with your impression so far of Shakespeare's Gaunt.

3 'An enforcèd pilgrimage'

Both Gaunt and Bullingbrook have already used the image of a pilgrimage in this scene. Find out where. References to pilgrimages and crusades occur throughout this play and also throughout the three sequel plays (see page 198). The desire to go on a pilgrimage or crusade will haunt Shakespeare's Bullingbrook until his death.

---

partial slander accusation of bias
looked when expected that
make . . . away sacrifice my own son
flourish fanfare
office function
dolour sadness

grief grievance, unhappiness
travail labour and travel
esteem consider, regard
foil metal setting for a jewel designed to show off its brilliance
journeyman a craftsman (one who has served his 'apprenticehood')

GAUNT Things sweet to taste prove in digestion sour.   235
   You urged me as a judge, but I had rather
   You would have bid me argue like a father.
   Oh, had it been a stranger, not my child,
   To smoothe his fault I should have been more mild.
   A partial slander sought I to avoid   240
   And in the sentence my own life destroyed.
   Alas, I looked when some of you should say
   I was too strict to make mine own away,
   But you gave leave to my unwilling tongue
   Against my will to do myself this wrong.   245
RICHARD Cousin, farewell, and uncle, bid him so.
   Six years we banish him and he shall go.   *Exit. Flourish*
AUMERLE Cousin, farewell. What presence must not know,
   From where you do remain let paper show.   [*Exit*]
MARSHAL My lord, no leave take I, for I will ride   250
   As far as land will let me by your side.
GAUNT Oh, to what purpose dost thou hoard thy words,
   That thou returnst no greeting to thy friends?
BULLINGBROOK I have too few to take my leave of you,
   When the tongue's office should be prodigal   255
   To breathe the abundant dolour of the heart.
GAUNT Thy grief is but thy absence for a time.
BULLINGBROOK Joy absent, grief is present for that time.
GAUNT What is six winters? They are quickly gone.
BULLINGBROOK To men in joy; but grief makes one hour ten.   260
GAUNT Call it a travail that thou tak'st for pleasure.
BULLINGBROOK My heart will sigh when I miscall it so,
   Which finds it an enforcèd pilgrimage.
GAUNT The sullen passage of thy weary steps
   Esteem as foil wherein thou art to set   265
   The precious jewel of thy home return.
BULLINGBROOK Nay, rather every tedious stride I make
   Will but remember me what a deal of world
   I wander from the jewels that I love.
   Must I not serve a long apprenticehood   270
   To foreign passages, and in the end,
   Having my freedom, boast of nothing else
   But that I was a journeyman to grief?

Gaunt's attempts to console his son meet with little success.
Bullingbrook goes into exile.

1 See the sweep of the whole scene
(in groups of eight or more)

To show the ebb and flow of this visually spectacular scene and to see how Shakespeare fills and empties his stage, devise a dumb show presentation.

Take the whole scene and decide all the major movements and gestures (remember to look for the internal stage directions). One of you must take notes. Now put the scripts down and, using the notes only, rehearse a dumb show or mime the scene. Try to create the atmosphere and the relationships of the actual scene. If you wish, use a few lines of your own at key points like 'Farewell', 'Let the battle begin', and so on.

Present your version to the rest of the class.

2 Your thoughts on Bullingbrook (in pairs)

This could be the last we see of Bullingbrook for some six years. Take alternate sentences of his final words (lines 293–308) and speak them to each other. As you speak the words, seize your partner by the wrist and shake it firmly whenever you say a strong or powerful word. What does Bullingbrook think of the power of imagination?

Bullingbrook describes himself as 'a true born Englishman'. Judging by the things that he and Mowbray have said and done, what qualities do you need to be a 'true born Englishman'? Is it possible to define what makes such a person today?

look what whatever
presence strewed the royal presence chamber with its floor covered with rushes
cloy surfeit, clog

fantastic imaginary
fell Sorrow deadly sorrow
lanceth not the sore does not cut deep enough to release the infection

GAUNT All places that the eye of heaven visits
    Are to a wise man ports and happy havens.   275
    Teach thy necessity to reason thus:
    There is no virtue like necessity.
    Think not the king did banish thee,
    But thou the king. Woe doth the heavier sit
    Where it perceives it is but faintly borne.   280
    Go, say I sent thee forth to purchase honour,
    And not the king exiled thee; or suppose
    Devouring pestilence hangs in our air
    And thou art flying to a fresher clime.
    Look what thy soul holds dear, imagine it   285
    To lie that way thou goest, not whence thou com'st.
    Suppose the singing birds musicians,
    The grass whereon thou treadst the presence strewed,
    The flowers fair ladies, and thy steps no more
    Than a delightful measure or a dance,   290
    For gnarling sorrow hath less power to bite
    The man that mocks at it and sets it light.
BULLINGBROOK Oh, who can hold a fire in his hand
    By thinking on the frosty Caucasus?
    Or cloy the hungry edge of appetite   295
    By bare imagination of a feast?
    Or wallow naked in December snow
    By thinking on fantastic summer's heat?
    Oh no, the apprehension of the good
    Gives but the greater feeling to the worse.   300
    Fell Sorrow's tooth doth never rankle more
    Than when he bites but lanceth not the sore.
GAUNT Come, come, my son, I'll bring thee on thy way.
    Had I thy youth and cause I would not stay.
BULLINGBROOK Then England's ground farewell, sweet soil adieu,   305
    My mother and my nurse that bears me yet.
    Where'er I wander, boast of this I can,
    Though banished, yet a true born Englishman.
               Exeunt

*Richard talks, in confidence, with his close associates
about the banished Bullingbrook.*

1 A different Richard (in groups of four)

Walk through the entry up to line 4 and try by your movements and
gestures to make sense of Richard's opening remark. What is
different about the king's entrance this time?

2 How do they speak? (in pairs)

Read lines 1–30 aloud, one as Richard, one as Aumerle, sitting face
to face at a desk or table. Find all the words connected with grief and
parting. What is the difference between the way Richard and Aumerle
use these words and the way Bullingbrook, Mowbray and the
Duchess of Gloucester talk in the previous scenes?

3 Richard's cronies

The men of Richard's court were
especially gaudy, with sleeves so long
they trailed along the ground. The
points of their shoes were usually far
longer than the feet themselves and
had to be held up by gold chains
stretched from the ends of the toes
to the knees.

If you were producing the play,
would you dress Bushy, Green and
Bagot in this manner?

---

rheum a watery discharge
for my heart because my heart
craft . . . grief the skill to pretend
  to be so overwhelmed with grief

our kinsman our kinsman
  Bullingbrook
underbearing enduring
affects affections

ACT 1   SCENE 4
The Court

Enter the King RICHARD *with* GREEN *and* BAGOT *at one door, and the*
Lord AUMERLE *at another*

RICHARD We did observe. Cousin Aumerle,
    How far brought you high Herford on his way?
AUMERLE I brought high Herford, if you call him so,
    But to the next highway, and there I left him.
RICHARD And say, what store of parting tears were shed? 5
AUMERLE Faith, none for me, except the northeast wind,
    Which then blew bitterly against our faces,
    Awaked the sleeping rheum and so by chance
    Did grace our hollow parting with a tear.
RICHARD What said our cousin when you parted with him? 10
AUMERLE 'Farewell',
    And, for my heart disdainèd that my tongue
    Should so profane the word, that taught me craft
    To counterfeit oppression of such grief
    That words seemed buried in my sorrow's grave. 15
    Marry, would the word 'farewell' have lengthened hours
    And added years to his short banishment,
    He should have had a volume of 'farewells'.
    But since it would not he had none of me.
RICHARD He is our cousin, cousin, but 'tis doubt, 20
    When time shall call him home from banishment,
    Whether our kinsman come to see his friends.
    Our self and Bushy, Bagot here and Green,
    Observed his courtship to the common people,
    How he did seem to dive into their hearts 25
    With humble and familiar courtesy,
    What reverence he did throw away on slaves,
    Wooing poor craftsmen with the craft of smiles
    And patient underbearing of his fortune,
    As 'twere to banish their affects with him. 30

*As Richard looks for ways to raise finances for his Irish wars,
news comes that Gaunt is seriously ill. Confiscating Gaunt's estates
will solve all his problems!*

1 'Cousinage, dangereux voisinage'
(Cousins, a dangerous closeness) (in pairs)

Bullingbrook was undoubtedly popular with the people. 40,000 Londoners turned out with tears and lamentations to watch his departure! One person reads lines 23–36 while the other mimes Bullingbrook's behaviour. Richard obviously dislikes his cousin's popularity with the common people. What do *you* think of Bullingbrook's behaviour?

2 Your feelings about Richard (in groups of three)

Take a part each and read this page sitting together around a table. Experiment with different ways of speaking Richard's final words. How attractive a character do you find Richard at this point in the play?

3 A handkerchief and mirror

The historical Richard is credited with introducing the handkerchief into noble society. Until then, courtiers had used their cuffs.

A recent production used a handkerchief and mirror as props for this scene. Think of ways in which they might have been used. Better still, actually rehearse and demonstrate it.

---

in reversion as an heir
next degree in hope hoped for
  successor to the crown
expedient ... made speedy
  measures must be taken

liberal largesse generosity in
  bestowing grants (see page 194)
**farm our royal realm/blank
  charters** methods of raising
  revenue (see page 194)
  subscribe them for put them
  down for

Off goes his bonnet to an oysterwench.
A brace of draymen bid God speed him well
And had the tribute of his supple knee,
With 'Thanks, my countrymen, my loving friends',
As were our England in reversion his,   35
And he our subjects' next degree in hope.
GREEN Well, he is gone, and with him go these thoughts.
Now, for the rebels which stand out in Ireland,
Expedient manage must be made, my liege,
Ere further leisure yield them further means   40
For their advantage and your highness' loss.
RICHARD We will ourself in person to this war,
And, for our coffers, with too great a court
And liberal largesse, are grown somewhat light,
We are enforced to farm our royal realm,   45
The revenue whereof shall furnish us
For our affairs in hand. If that come short
Our substitutes at home shall have blank charters
Whereto when they shall know what men are rich
They shall subscribe them for large sums of gold   50
And send them after to supply our wants,
For we will make for Ireland presently.

Enter BUSHY.

Bushy, what news?
BUSHY Old John of Gaunt is grievous sick, my lord,
Suddenly taken, and hath sent post haste   55
To entreat your majesty to visit him.
RICHARD Where lies he?
BUSHY   At Ely House.
RICHARD Now put it, God, in the physician's mind
To help him to his grave immediately.
The lining of his coffers shall make coats   60
To deck our soldiers for these Irish wars.
Come, gentlemen, let's all go visit him.
Pray God we may make haste and come too late.
[ALL] Amen.
                                                                        Exeunt

43

Looking back at Act 1

The king seems to be supreme. Gaunt, the most powerful man in England after the king, is dying. Bullingbrook, his son and heir, is banished, leaving his lands at the king's mercy. The problem of Mowbray's loyalty has also been resolved by his perpetual banishment.

1 A cartoon version

Make a cartoon drawing for each of the four scenes of Act 1 which shows the central action of that scene (draw matchstick men and women if your artistic skills are a little shaky). Write a caption for each drawing.

2 Turn the play into a novel

Write the events of Act 1 Scene 1 as the first chapter of a novel. Describe the setting, atmosphere, characters, inner thoughts and so on. Your dialogue should also suggest the attitudes and manners of this society.

3 How ambitious is Bullingbrook?

Look back through Act 1 and find all the words or images to do with 'height'. How many of them are used by or of Bullingbrook?

4 Design a shield

Many productions have emphasised the colour and splendour of this medieval world. Design an heraldic shield for one of the major characters so far seen (Richard, Gaunt, Bullingbrook, Mowbray) or for the dead Gloucester. There are references in Scene 1 to some of the heraldic emblems that they used, but you may prefer to design a more modern version. Try to capture something of your character's status and personality. Show your shield to others in the class and ask them to guess to whom it belongs.

5 Be a reporter

Write newspaper articles (one for a tabloid and one for a 'heavy') reporting the events of the Trial by Combat. Include headlines and photographs. You could also write the editorials for the same papers (one pro-Richard, one pro-Bullingbrook).

6 Ways of staging the Trial by Combat

In our perhaps more civilised age it is difficult to imagine what a Trial by Combat was like. Perhaps the nearest modern equivalent is a world heavyweight boxing championship.

In groups of six or eight work out the basic movements for 1.3.1–120 and present the Combat as if it were a boxing match (Lord Marshal = referee? King Richard = ringside judge?). Don't forget the rituals of being called to the centre, staring out your opponent, flexing muscles and so on. Present your version to the rest of the class who can act as ringside spectators and supporters. Does this activity add anything to your understanding of the Trial by Combat?

One early twentieth-century production used live horses for this scene, much to the consternation of the front rows of the stalls! How would you stage the Combat?

7 Looking forward to Act 2

So far we have really only seen the public face of Richard and what we glimpse of the private Richard in Act 1 Scene 4 is certainly not very flattering. See how much sympathy you feel for him in Act 2 and note the use he makes of his newly acquired political advantage.

Remember that events in Act 2 Scene 1 are viewed very much through the eyes of the nobles, many of them anxious about their own powers and privileges. Decide how much truth there is in the dying Gaunt's powerful denunciations of the king's misgovernment. York, Northumberland, Ross and Willoughby will also have much to say on this. How valid are their criticisms?

Gaunt, close to death, wishes to warn the king of the foolishness of his conduct. His brother York doubts whether Richard will pay any heed.

---

1 The end of an era (in groups of four)

The great age of King Edward III is coming to an end. These two old men are his last surviving sons. Take a sentence each and read lines 1–30. What emotions do you sense in their words?

2 Hearing the music, feeling the pain (in pairs)

a Hearing the music

Can you hear the patterns in Gaunt's words (lines 5–16)? Read the lines, taking a half-line each and handing over to your partner. Make up your mind as you read when you are going to hand over to your partner. Then let your partner start each line. Such a pause or break in the middle of the verse line is called a **caesura**.

Now concentrate on seeing any **antitheses** (contrasting of thoughts or ideas) in these lines. Sit facing each other and read the lines together, but change seats with each new contrast. Talk about your disagreements!

b Feeling the pain

Gaunt is dying. On the Elizabethan stage he would probably have been carried onto the stage in a litter. Try to feel Gaunt's pain and struggling for breath by doing press-ups as you read these lines. You can place the script on the ground in front of you. If you are not fit enough for press-ups, do step-ups on a chair.

Talk about which quality (the music or the pain) should be felt most at this point. Or is it possible to feel both?

---

unstaid youth wild youthfulness
glose talk superficially
metres verses
proud Italy the traditional source of folly and wickedness for the Elizabethans (Richard's court in fact followed French fashions)

tardy-apish copying something which is long out of date
so it be so long as it is
will . . . regard desire will not obey reason or common sense

ACT 2 SCENE 1
Ely House

Enter JOHN OF GAUNT, sick, with the DUKE OF YORK, etc.

GAUNT Will the king come that I may breathe my last
    In wholesome counsel to his unstaid youth?
YORK Vex not yourself, nor strive not with your breath,
    For all in vain comes counsel to his ear.
GAUNT Oh, but they say the tongues of dying men   5
    Enforce attention like deep harmony.
    Where words are scarce they are seldom spent in vain,
    For they breathe truth that breathe their words in pain.
    He that no more must say is listened more
    Than they whom youth and ease have taught to glose.   10
    More are men's ends marked than their lives before.
    The setting sun, and music at the close,
    As the last taste of sweets, is sweetest last,
    Writ in remembrance more than things long past.
    Though Richard my life's counsel would not hear   15
    My death's sad tale may yet undeaf his ear.
YORK No, it is stopped with other flattering sounds,
    As praises, of whose taste the wise are fond,
    Lascivious metres, to whose venom sound
    The open ear of youth doth always listen,   20
    Report of fashions in proud Italy,
    Whose manners still our tardy-apish nation
    Limps after in base imitation.
    Where doth the world thrust forth a vanity –
    So it be new there's no respect how vile –   25
    That is not quickly buzzed into his ears?
    Then all too late comes counsel to be heard
    Where will doth mutiny with wit's regard.
    Direct not him whose way himself will choose.
    'Tis breath thou lackst and that breath wilt thou lose.   30

Gaunt passionately evokes a picture of the England he once knew and bitterly compares it with its present condition.

1 'A prophet new inspired' (in groups of three)

There are many visions of England in the play. It is the object of deepest love and concern and no one feels this more than Gaunt. His thoughts here are built around a single contrast (antithesis) which can be summed up briefly as 'England then and now'. His thoughts unfold (as they do in many of Shakespeare's longer speeches) in three stages. Decide where you think the three stages are and read Gaunt's speech taking a stage each (hint: a change of thought may not necessarily coincide with the end of a sentence).

2 The ideal past (in groups of six to eight)

Choose lines or phrases that you think most powerfully express Gaunt's vision of England's greatness and speak them to each other. Then use these phrases as part of a modern party political broadcast.

3 The shameful present

Remember Gaunt's bond (1.1.2) and think about the picture suggested by line 64. If 'royal kings' and a 'happy breed of men' once ruled England, who now seems to be in control? Read page 194. Which of Richard's methods of raising finance does Gaunt seem to be referring to here?

4 Crusades

For Gaunt (lines 52–6), England's former greatness lay in its crusading kings. The 'sepulchre in stubborn Jewry' refers to Christ's tomb in the holy city of Jerusalem which the Crusaders sought to recapture from the Muslims. Crusades were a kind of military pilgrimage.

---

betimes soon . . . early
insatiate ravenous, insatiable
consuming means devouring its food supply
demi-paradise one of two paradises
office function, purpose

world's ransom Christ's death was the ransom which paid for mankind's sins
leased out 'farmed' (see page 194)
tenement or pelting farm rented smallholding or worthless farm

GAUNT Methinks I am a prophet new inspired,
And thus expiring do foretell of him.
His rash fierce blaze of riot cannot last,
For violent fires soon burn out themselves.
Small showers last long but sudden storms are short.   35
He tires betimes that spurs too fast betimes.
With eager feeding food doth choke the feeder.
Light vanity, insatiate cormorant,
Consuming means, soon preys upon itself.
This royal throne of kings, this sceptred isle,   40
This earth of majesty, this seat of Mars,
This other Eden, demi-paradise,
This fortress built by Nature for herself
Against infection and the hand of war,
This happy breed of men, this little world,   45
This precious stone set in the silver sea
Which serves it in the office of a wall
Or as a moat defensive to a house
Against the envy of less happier lands,
This blessèd plot, this earth, this realm, this England,   50
This nurse, this teeming womb of royal kings
Feared by their breed and famous by their birth,
Renownèd for their deeds as far from home
For Christian service and true chivalry
As is the sepulchre in stubborn Jewry   55
Of the world's ransom, blessèd Mary's son,
This land of such dear souls, this dear, dear land,
Dear for her reputation through the world,
Is now leased out, I die pronouncing it,
Like to a tenement or pelting farm.   60
England, bound in with the triumphant sea
Whose rocky shore beats back the envious siege
Of watery Neptune, is now bound in with shame,
With inky blots and rotten parchment bonds,
That England that was wont to conquer others   65
Hath made a shameful conquest of itself.
Ah, would the scandal vanish with my life,
How happy then were my ensuing death!

Richard and his court come to visit the dying Gaunt.

---

1 Gaunt's bitterness (in pairs)

Look at Gaunt's first assault on Richard (lines 73–83). Take alternate lines and read this section through slowly and loudly. Then one person reads while the other echoes all the lean, bony, ill/sick/dying words. Finally, read it in unison stressing very powerfully every possible example of such word-play. For example:

'Watching **breeds leanness, leanness** is **all gaunt**'

Talk about the effect you feel these lines might have on Richard.

Now read lines 84–103, one of you as Gaunt and one as Richard. Whenever you say words relating to yourself pat your chest. Whenever you say words relating to your partner prod him very firmly. Who wins?

2 Youth and age (in groups of six to eight)

Rehearse and present to the rest of the class a staging of lines 69–103. Richard and his court could behave as if they were a group of rather impolite young people visiting an old, rich relative. The non-speakers should use no scripts, but instead react and comment in role.

3 'A thousand flatterers sit within thy crown'

Read and think about lines 100–03. Draw a picture of the image you have in your mind. You will find echoes of this image later in the play.

---

nicely delicately, trivially
anointed body at his coronation, the king's body was anointed with holy oil (see also 1.2.38). Richard refers to this in 3.2.54–7

compass boundary
verge border
the waste the destruction (that 'the thousand flatterers' are causing)

Enter King RICHARD, QUEEN, AUMERLE, BUSHY, GREEN, BAGOT, ROSS
and WILLOUGHBY

YORK The king is come. Deal mildly with his youth,
    For young hot colts being reined do rage the more.   70
QUEEN How fares our noble uncle Lancaster?
RICHARD What comfort, man? How is't with agèd Gaunt?
GAUNT Oh, how that name befits my composition!
    Old Gaunt indeed, and gaunt in being old.
    Within me grief hath kept a tedious fast,   75
    And who abstains from meat that is not gaunt?
    For sleeping England long time have I watched.
    Watching breeds leanness; leanness is all gaunt.
    The pleasure that some fathers feed upon
    Is my strict fast, I mean my children's looks,   80
    And therein fasting hast thou made me gaunt.
    Gaunt am I for the grave, gaunt as a grave,
    Whose hollow womb inherits naught but bones.
RICHARD Can sick men play so nicely with their names?
GAUNT No, misery makes sport to mock itself.   85
    Since thou dost seek to kill my name in me
    I mock my name, great king, to flatter thee.
RICHARD Should dying men flatter with those that live?
GAUNT No, no, men living flatter those that die.
RICHARD Thou now a-dying sayest thou flatterest me.   90
GAUNT Oh no, thou diest, though I the sicker be.
RICHARD I am in health, I breathe, and see thee ill.
GAUNT Now He that made me knows I see thee ill,
    Ill in myself to see, and in thee, seeing ill.
    Thy deathbed is no lesser than thy land,   95
    Wherein thou liest in reputation sick,
    And thou, too careless patient as thou art,
    Commit'st thy anointed body to the cure
    Of those physicians that first wounded thee.
    A thousand flatterers sit within thy crown   100
    Whose compass is no bigger than thy head,
    And yet encagèd in so small a verge
    The waste is no whit lesser than thy land.

Gaunt's rebukes provoke Richard to anger. Gaunt is carried off to his bed.

---

1 Confrontation and accusation (in groups of eight or more)

Gaunt is angry and the historical Richard was well-known for his outbursts of rage. Divide into a Richard group and a Gaunt group. Choose a line/phrase from lines 93–140 that best expresses your character's anger and memorise it. Then sit facing your opposing group and hurl your words at them. Try it in different ways – perhaps first hiss your anger, then build up into a crescendo of rage.

What are the accusations that Gaunt makes against Richard and which one is he making here?

2 Edward's sons

Use the family tree on page 192 to sort out the relationships that Gaunt refers to in lines 124–31.

---

bondslave bound by legal bonds
ague's feverish man's
admonition reproof, rebuke
pelican young pelicans were
  supposed to feed on the blood of
  their mother. What grim meaning

does Gaunt create in lines 126–31
  using this image?
tapped out drawn out like a drink
  from a barrel
unkindness unnatural feelings
sullens sulks

Oh, had thy grandsire with a prophet's eye
Seen how his son's son should destroy his sons,   105
From forth thy reach he would have laid thy shame,
Deposing thee before thou wert possessed,
Which art possessed now to depose thyself.
Why cousin, wert thou regent of the world
It were a shame to let this land by lease,   110
But for thy world enjoying but this land
Is it not more than shame to shame it so?
Landlord of England art thou now, not king,
Thy state of law is bondslave to the law,
And thou –

RICHARD   A lunatic lean-witted fool,   115
Presuming on an ague's privilege,
Dar'st with thy frozen admonition
Make pale our cheek, chasing the royal blood
With fury from his native residence.
Now, by my seat's right royal majesty,   120
Wert thou not brother to great Edward's son
This tongue that runs so roundly in thy head
Should run thy head from thy unreverent shoulders.

GAUNT Oh spare me not, my brother Edward's son,
For that I was his father Edward's son.   125
That blood already, like the pelican,
Hast thou tapped out and drunkenly caroused.
My brother Gloucester, plain well-meaning soul,
Whom fair befall in heaven 'mongst happy souls,
May be a precedent and witness good   130
That thou respect'st not spilling Edward's blood.
Join with the present sickness that I have
And thy unkindness be like crooked age
To crop at once a too long withered flower.
Live in thy shame, but die not shame with thee.   135
These words hereafter thy tormentors be.
Convey me to my bed, then to my grave.
Love they to live that love and honour have.   *Exit*

RICHARD And let them die that age and sullens have,
For both hast thou, and both become the grave.   140

News comes of Gaunt's death. Richard announces that he will take over all of Gaunt's possessions. York can bear Richard's behaviour no longer.

1 A crucial decision (in groups of three)

English kings had confiscated lands before. Richard himself had appropriated Gloucester's possessions. Seizing Gaunt's vast Lancastrian estates would greatly ease Richard's financial problems and remove a powerful rival. But it was a technical act of tyranny, putting the king's will above the law.

Decide how much thought Richard seems to give to the matter. Take a part each and read lines 141–64. Does Richard's decision seem carefully planned or done on the spur of the moment?

2 Another lecture! (in pairs)

The play is full of uncles. Richard must be heartily sick of them. Gaunt had been Richard's counsellor since his coronation at the age of ten. Gloucester had been a thorn in his flesh. Now York! In one production, after lines 160–63, Richard placed his hands over his ears in expectation of the outburst he knew was going to come!

York, however, talks to his king in a rather different manner to Gaunt. Speak lines 163–85 to each other. Take it in turns to be York. Try it in two ways:

a as if you were a wife reproaching a useless husband who has just done something wrong – yet again

b as if you were a teacher telling off your favourite student for improper behaviour.

What four words would you use to describe the tone of York's speech?

---

kern foot-soldiers
venom . . . no venom else since there are no snakes in Ireland the Irish are the only poisonous creatures there

prevention of poor Bullingbrook about his marriage when Bullingbrook was in exile the historical Richard did indeed stop the marriage. Why do you think it is mentioned here?

YORK I do beseech your majesty, impute his words
     To wayward sickliness and age in him.
     He loves you, on my life, and holds you dear
     As Harry Duke of Herford were he here.
RICHARD Right, you say true. As Herford's love, so his.   145
     As theirs, so mine, and all be as it is.

Enter NORTHUMBERLAND.

NORTHUMBERLAND My liege, old Gaunt commends him to your
          majesty.
RICHARD What says he?
NORTHUMBERLAND   Nay nothing, all is said.
     His tongue is now a stringless instrument.
     Words, life and all old Lancaster hath spent.   150
YORK Be York the next that must be bankrupt so.
     Though death be poor it ends a mortal woe.
RICHARD The ripest fruit first falls, and so doth he.
     His time is spent, our pilgrimage must be.
     So much for that. Now, for our Irish wars,   155
     We must supplant those rough rug-headed kern,
     Which live like venom where no venom else
     But only they have privilege to live.
     And, for these great affairs do ask some charge,
     Towards our assistance we do seize to us   160
     The plate, coin, revenues and moveables
     Whereof our uncle Gaunt did stand possessed.
YORK How long shall I be patient? Ah, how long
     Shall tender duty make me suffer wrong?
     Not Gloucester's death nor Herford's banishment,   165
     Nor Gaunt's rebukes, nor England's private wrongs,
     Nor the prevention of poor Bullingbrook
     About his marriage, nor my own disgrace
     Have ever made me sour my patient cheek
     Or bend one wrinkle on my sovereign's face.   170
     I am the last of noble Edward's sons,
     Of whom thy father, Prince of Wales, was first.
     In war was never lion raged more fierce,
     In peace was never gentle lamb more mild
     Than was that young and princely gentleman.   175

*York cites Richard's father, the Black Prince, as an example of the right
conduct for a king and warns Richard of the consequences of seizing
Bullingbrook's inheritance.*

1 The nature of the feudal contract (in pairs)

York's words (lines 186–208) make abundantly clear the enormity of
what Richard proposes, at least as far as the nobles are concerned.
The feudal contract worked both ways. Subjects owed loyalty to their
king, but a king had a duty to uphold the rights of his subjects.

Feel how York's words echo this sense of mutual fairness and
obligation. Sit at a table and take up arm-wrestling positions. Read
the lines through, handing over to your partner at each full stop or
semi-colon. Try to force down your partner's arm but only when you
are actually speaking. Swap lines and do it again.

2 Try to persuade your king (in groups of six)

In the last years of his reign Richard became increasingly remote.
One chronicler records how he took to sitting alone after dinner on a
high throne, surrounded by silent courtiers. Any man who met the
king's gaze was obliged to kneel.

One person speaks lines 186–208 to Richard. The rest of the
group forms a silent barrier to prevent the speaker from getting near
the king. Try it again, but this time the 'guards' echo words and
phrases in a hostile or jeering fashion.

3 Are you being manipulated?

Is Shakespeare, through the characters of Gaunt and York, presenting us with a particularly one-sided view of Richard here?

---

royalties titles
take from time . . . rights all
agreements and laws of inheritance
will disappear completely (the 'his'
refers to 'time')
ensue follow

**letters patents/sue his livery/
deny his offered
homage** references to the legal
process by which the absent
Bullingbrook would have had to
claim his inheritance

His face thou hast, for even so looked he,
Accomplished with the number of thy hours.
But when he frowned it was against the French
And not against his friends. His noble hand
Did win what he did spend, and spent not that   180
Which his triumphant father's hand had won.
His hands were guilty of no kindred blood
But bloody with the enemies of his kin.
Oh, Richard! York is too far gone with grief,
Or else he never would compare between.   185
RICHARD Why, uncle, what's the matter?
YORK   O my liege,
Pardon me if you please; if not, I, pleased
Not to be pardoned, am content with all.
Seek you to seize and gripe into your hands
The royalties and rights of banished Herford?   190
Is not Gaunt dead? And doth not Herford live?
Was not Gaunt just? And is not Harry true?
Did not the one deserve to have an heir?
Is not his heir a well-deserving son?
Take Herford's rights away and take from time   195
His charters and his customary rights.
Let not tomorrow then ensue today.
Be not thyself. For how art thou a king
But by fair sequence and succession?
Now, afore God – God forbid I say true –   200
If you do wrongfully seize Herford's rights,
Call in the letters patents that he hath
By his attorneys-general to sue
His livery, and deny his offered homage,
You pluck a thousand dangers on your head,   205
You lose a thousand well-disposèd hearts,
And prick my tender patience to those thoughts
Which honour and allegiance cannot think.
RICHARD Think what you will, we seize into our hands
His plate, his goods, his money and his lands.   210
YORK I'll not be by the while. My liege, farewell.
What will ensue hereof there's none can tell,
But by bad courses may be understood
That their events can never fall out good.   *Exit*

Richard departs for Ireland, leaving York as Governor of England in his absence. The lords of Northumberland, Ross and Willoughby discuss events.

---

1 The king's departure (in groups of six or more)

Work on a staging of Richard's exit (lines 215–23) in a way that reflects his behaviour generally in this scene. Use the reactions and behaviour of the members of his court (Aumerle, Bushy, Green, Bagot, Ross, Willoughby, Northumberland) to help you here. Show your version to the rest of the class.

2 Feel the danger (in groups of five or more)

Three lords are left alone. They are clearly unhappy, but to voice your fears of the king is to risk being accused of treason (as indeed happened to Mowbray).

Three readers should stand or sit in the centre while the rest make a circle of chairs around them including a number of empty chairs. As the lords speak lines 224–45, the others should stand up at random moments and walk to a new seat. As soon as the lords notice a movement they must stop speaking and only continue when the circle is seated again. See if you can create a sense of fear and conspiracy in the voices of the three lords.

3 Your thoughts on Richard?

We do not see Richard again until Act 3 when he returns from Ireland. Write down the four words or phrases which you feel best sum him up at this point. Compare this with your picture of him at the end of 1.1 and 1.3.

I trow I believe
disburdened unburdened
liberal free, unrestrained
tends ... to does what you would
  say refer (favourably) to

bereft, and gelded of his
  patrimony denied and deprived
  of his inheritance
many mo many more
merely purely

RICHARD Go, Bushy, to the Earl of Wiltshire straight.   215
            Bid him repair to us to Ely House
            To see this business. Tomorrow next
            We will for Ireland, and 'tis time, I trow.
            And we create in absence of ourself
            Our uncle York lord governor of England,   220
            For he is just, and always loved us well.
            Come on, our queen; tomorrow must we part.
            Be merry, for our time of stay is short.
                        Exeunt King Richard and Queen,
                        Aumerle, Bushy, Green and Bagot
NORTHUMBERLAND Well, lords, the Duke of Lancaster is dead.
ROSS And living too, for now his son is duke.   225
WILLOUGHBY Barely in title, not in revenues.
NORTHUMBERLAND Richly in both if justice had her right.
ROSS My heart is great, but it must break with silence
            Ere't be disburdened with a liberal tongue.
NORTHUMBERLAND Nay, speak thy mind, and let him ne'er speak
            more   230
            That speaks thy words again to do thee harm.
WILLOUGHBY Tends that that thou wouldst speak to the Duke of
            Herford?
            If it be so, out with it boldly, man.
            Quick is mine ear to hear of good towards him.
ROSS No good at all that I can do for him,   235
            Unless you call it good to pity him,
            Bereft, and gelded of his patrimony.
NORTHUMBERLAND Now afore God 'tis shame such wrongs are borne
            In him, a royal prince, and many mo
            Of noble blood in this declining land.   240
            The king is not himself, but basely led
            By flatterers, and what they will inform
            Merely in hate 'gainst any of us all
            That will the king severely prosecute
            'Gainst us, our lives, our children and our heirs.   245

The lords give vent to their anger and fear.

---

1 What are the lords' complaints?

Like Gaunt and York, these nobles are most concerned about Richard's government of the country.

Make a list of all the things that the lords are unhappy about and decide what seems to be their greatest concern. Are their complaints any different to those expressed by the other two lords, Gaunt and York, earlier in the scene?

2 Do they dare trust each other? (in groups of five to seven)

Sit together around a table. Three of you read lines 224–76 slowly, pausing at the end of each statement or sentence, at which point the rest must respond with either ''Tis shame such wrongs are borne' or 'Speak thy mind'. Decide which of the three men you think takes the lead in this conversation.

3 'The hollow eyes of death'

Read lines 270–72. Close your eyes and try to visualise the image Northumberland creates. Write it down or draw it.

---

the commons the House of Commons (which in those days represented only the gentry and wealthy merchants)
pilled plundered, pillaged
fined/blanks/exactions/ benevolences/the realm in

farm (methods of raising money – see page 194)
I wot not I know not
strike furl (or roll up) the sails to weather out a storm (but is there another meaning?)

ROSS The commons hath he pilled with grievous taxes
       And quite lost their hearts. The nobles hath he fined
       For ancient quarrels and quite lost their hearts.
WILLOUGHBY And daily new exactions are devised,
       As blanks, benevolences, and I wot not what.   250
       But what a God's name doth become of this?
NORTHUMBERLAND Wars hath not wasted it, for warred he hath
       not,
       But basely yielded upon compromise
       That which his ancestors achieved with blows.
       More hath he spent in peace than they in wars.   255
ROSS The Earl of Wiltshire hath the realm in farm.
WILLOUGHBY The king grown bankrupt like a broken man.
NORTHUMBERLAND Reproach and dissolution hangeth over him.
ROSS He hath not money for these Irish wars,
       His burthenous taxations notwithstanding,   260
       But by the robbing of the banished duke.
NORTHUMBERLAND His noble kinsman, most degenerate king!
       But lords, we hear this fearful tempest sing
       Yet seek no shelter to avoid the storm.
       We see the wind sit sore upon our sails   265
       And yet we strike not but securely perish.
ROSS We see the very wreck that we must suffer,
       And unavoided is the danger now
       For suffering so the causes of our wreck.
NORTHUMBERLAND Not so. Even through the hollow eyes of death 270
       I spy life peering, but I dare not say
       How near the tidings of our comfort is.
WILLOUGHBY Nay, let us share thy thoughts as thou dost ours.
ROSS Be confident to speak, Northumberland.
       We three are but thy self, and speaking so   275
       Thy words are but as thoughts. Therefore be bold.

Northumberland reveals the news that Bullingbrook is making his way back to England with his supporters.

1 An impressive list (in small groups)

Northumberland's account of the leading figures in Bullingbrook's tiny force of just 3,000 men makes interesting reading. Norbery, Erpingham and Waterton had accompanied Bullingbrook on military expeditions against the heathens of Lithuania in 1390 and 1392, which was probably where their bonds of loyalty were first forged. The Earl of Arundel (whose son is mentioned here) was executed by Richard for joining the Gloucester faction, and his brother removed from his post as Archbishop of Canterbury for the same reason. The factions opposing Richard are now gathering around Bullingbrook.

Divide Northumberland's speech into sections and read parts of it in turn. As you take over from the previous person, try to convey the sense of mounting excitement. Decide whether this approach works for Northumberland's final sentence (lines 297–8).

2 Show Northumberland's vision of the future
(in groups of three or four)

In lines 291–6, Northumberland paints a picture of what he hopes their rebellion will achieve. Choose a line and mime it to the others who must guess which line it is you have chosen.

Is it possible to tell if Northumberland is actually proposing to dethrone Richard or merely to replace his ministers?

Brittaine Brittany
expedience speed
had ere this would have done before now
imp out repair (a term from falconry)
broking pawn pawnbrokers, money lenders

in post in haste
Ravenspurgh a port on the Humber (Bullingbrook's most loyal support lay in the north-east)
hold out my horse if my horse lasts out

NORTHUMBERLAND Then thus: I have from le Port Blanc,
      A bay in Brittaine, received intelligence
      That Harry Duke of Herford, Rainold Lord Cobham,
      [The son of Richard Earl of Arundel]   280
      That late broke from the Duke of Exeter,
      His brother, Archbishop late of Canterbury,
      Sir Thomas Erpingham, Sir John Ramston,
      Sir John Norbery, Sir Robert Waterton, and Francis Coint,
      All these well furnished by the Duke of Brittaine   285
      With eight tall ships, three thousand men of war,
      Are making hither with all due expedience
      And shortly mean to touch our northern shore.
      Perhaps they had ere this, but that they stay
      The first departing of the king for Ireland.   290
      If then we shall shake off our slavish yoke,
      Imp out our drooping country's broken wing,
      Redeem from broking pawn the blemished crown,
      Wipe off the dust that hides our sceptre's gilt,
      And make high majesty look like itself,   295
      Away with me in post to Ravenspurgh.
      But if you faint, as fearing to do so,
      Stay and be secret, and myself will go.
ROSS To horse, to horse! Urge doubts to them that fear.
WILLOUGHBY Hold out my horse, and I will first be there.   300

                                            Exeunt

The queen waits uneasily for the return of her husband.

1 Different perspectives

Where Northumberland sees the departure of a 'degenerate king', the queen here genuinely grieves for her 'sweet Richard'. The notion of different perspectives is crucial to the play and Bushy offers us an interesting insight in lines 14–27 where he ingeniously plays with this idea. A fuller explanation is given on pages 186–7.

Holbein's *The Ambassadors* (a famous example of a 'perspective' picture). 'Perspectives' is the name given to pictures which appear distorted when viewed from the front ('rightly') but show a clear image ('distinguish form') when viewed from an angle ('eyed awry'). What is the distorted slanting image in the centre foreground of Holbein's picture? (See page 186.) What connection might it have with Bushy's words (lines 18–20)?

ACT 2 · SCENE 2
Windsor Castle

Enter the QUEEN, BUSHY, BAGOT

BUSHY Madam, your majesty is too much sad.
    You promised, when you parted with the king,
    To lay aside life-harming heaviness
    And entertain a cheerful disposition.
QUEEN To please the king I did. To please myself   5
    I cannot do it; yet I know no cause
    Why I should welcome such a guest as grief
    Save bidding farewell to so sweet a guest
    As my sweet Richard. Yet again methinks
    Some unborn sorrow ripe in Fortune's womb   10
    Is coming towards me, and my inward soul
    With nothing trembles; at some thing it grieves,
    More than with parting from my lord the king.
BUSHY Each substance of a grief hath twenty shadows
    Which shows like grief itself but is not so,   15
    For sorrow's eye, glazèd with blinding tears,
    Divides one thing entire to many objects,
    Like perspectives, which rightly gazed upon
    Show nothing but confusion; eyed awry
    Distinguish form. So your sweet majesty,   20
    Looking awry upon your lord's departure,
    Find shapes of grief more than himself to wail
    Which, looked on as it is, is naught but shadows
    Of what it is not. Then, thrice-gracious queen,
    More than your lord's departure weep not. More's not
        seen,   25
    Or if it be 'tis with false sorrow's eye
    Which for things true weeps things imaginary.
QUEEN It may be so, but yet my inward soul
    Persuades me it is otherwise. Howe'er it be
    I cannot but be sad, so heavy sad   30
    As, though on thinking on no thought I think,
    Makes me with heavy nothing faint and shrink.

*Green enters with news that Bullingbrook has returned to England and
many English lords are flocking to join him.*

1 The private world of queen and courtiers (in pairs)

The court of Richard II was criticised for extravagance and deca-
dence, but renowned, too, for artistic excellence and a love of beauty
and culture. Geoffrey Chaucer read his poems to Richard's court.

Read lines 1–40 to each other slowly and clearly. Echo any word or
phrase which suggests sorrow or foreboding. Compare your impressions here of Richard's 'cronies' with your reactions to them in 1.4
and 2.1.

2 The plights of individuals (in groups of three to five)

The play is not just about the great historical event of Richard's
downfall and the actions of the two great protagonists, Richard and
Bullingbrook. It also focuses on the reactions and fates of the many
lesser people caught up in events. This scene shows how these people
cope.

Work on lines 38–66. Three of you take the parts of the queen,
Bushy and Bagot (others can be ladies- or gentlemen-in-waiting).
Rehearse a presentation to the rest of the class which highlights the
reactions of each individual to the disastrous news. Explore the
different ways in which Green might enter.

3 'A gasping new-delivered mother'

How many other examples can you find from lines 1–66 of images
which echo or parallel this line? What do they all suggest?

---

conceit imagination. The queen
(lines 34–40) says that even an
imaginary sorrow has an underlying
cause, but her sorrow seems born
of nothing at all
'tis in reversion ... possess it is
as if I am waiting to inherit my
sorrow from someone else

I wot I think
retired brought back
revolted faction party of rebels
staff staff of office
prodigy unnatural thing,
monstrous child

BUSHY 'Tis nothing but conceit, my gracious lady.

QUEEN 'Tis nothing less. Conceit is still derived
    From some forefather grief. Mine is not so,   35
    For nothing hath begot my something grief,
    Or something hath the nothing that I grieve.
    'Tis in reversion that I do possess,
    But what it is that is not yet known what
    I cannot name; 'tis nameless woe I wot.   40

Enter GREEN.

GREEN God save your majesty, and well met, gentlemen.
    I hope the king is not yet shipped for Ireland.

QUEEN Why hopest thou so? 'Tis better hope he is,
    For his designs crave haste, his haste good hope;
    Then wherefore dost thou hope he is not shipped?   45

GREEN That he, our hope, might have retired his power
    And driven into despair an enemy's hope
    Who strongly hath set footing in this land.
    The banished Bullingbrook repeals himself
    And with uplifted arms is safe arrived   50
    At Ravenspurgh.

QUEEN   Now God in heaven forbid!

GREEN Ah madam, 'tis too true; and that is worse
    The Lord Northumberland, his son young Harry Percy,
    The lords of Ross, Beaumond and Willoughby,
    With all their powerful friends are fled to him.   55

BUSHY Why have you not proclaimed Northumberland
    And all the rest, revolted faction, traitors?

GREEN We have, whereupon the Earl of Worcester
    Hath broke his staff, resigned his stewardship,
    And all the Household servants fled with him   60
    To Bullingbrook.

QUEEN So, Green, thou art the midwife to my woe
    And Bullingbrook my sorrow's dismal heir.
    Now hath my soul brought forth her prodigy
    And I, a gasping new-delivered mother,   65
    Have woe to woe, sorrow to sorrow joined.

York prepares for war.

1 The queen and her world

Does this resemble your idea of the queen in this scene? Decide whom you would cast in the part **a** from TV, films or theatre **b** from your class, school or college.

cozening deceiving
bands bonds
signs of war a gorget or metal collar
surfeit excesses
try test
your son Aumerle

which way whichever way
the commons cold the House of Commons hostile, unsupportive
sirrah . . . knave both customary forms of address to servants
presently immediately

BUSHY Despair not, madam.
QUEEN   Who shall hinder me?
          I will despair, and be at enmity
          With cozening hope. He is a flatterer,
          A parasite, a keeper-back of death   70
          Who gently would dissolve the bands of life
          Which false hope lingers in extremity.

Enter YORK.

GREEN Here comes the Duke of York.
QUEEN With signs of war about his agèd neck.
          Oh, full of careful business are his looks!   75
          Uncle, for God's sake speak comfortable words.
YORK Should I do so I should belie my thoughts.
          Comfort's in heaven and we are on the earth
          Where nothing lives but crosses, cares and grief.
          Your husband, he is gone to save far off   80
          Whilst others come to make him lose at home.
          Here am I left to underprop his land
          Who weak with age cannot support myself.
          Now comes the sick hour that his surfeit made,
          Now shall he try his friends that flattered him.   85

Enter a SERVINGMAN.

SERVINGMAN My lord, your son was gone before I came.
YORK He was? Why so, go all which way it will.
          The nobles they are fled, the commons cold,
          And will, I fear, revolt on Herford's side.
          Sirrah, get thee to Plashy, to my sister Gloucester.   90
          Bid her send me presently a thousand pound.
          Hold, take my ring.
SERVINGMAN My lord, I had forgot to tell your lordship.
          Today as I came by I callèd there –
          But I shall grieve you to report the rest.   95
YORK What is't, knave?
SERVINGMAN An hour before I came the duchess died.

*York begins the task of mustering loyal supporters to resist the invasion.
He leaves with the queen for Berkeley Castle.*

1 Catch York's mood (in groups of six)

Each person chooses a line or phrase from this page which reveals
York's mood or temperament. Memorise your line and walk around
saying it to the others as if you were York. Decide which line seems to
sum York up best.

Next read the speech through, taking a sentence each in turn. After
each sentence the group must describe York's mood at that moment.

Now put the whole speech into context. Set up your group to
represent the characters here (queen, Bushy, Green, Bagot, servingman) plus two chairs to represent Richard and Bullingbrook. One
person reads York's speech, addressing every line or phrase to
someone (or something) in the group. Can you see York's mood as
well as hear it?

2 Brothers and sisters

Decide which brother York refers to in line 102. Can you find
anything earlier in the scene to explain why he mistakenly calls the
queen 'sister' in line 105?

---

so my untruth . . . to it so long as
my disloyalty had not been the
cause
posts messengers

somewhat we must do we must
do something
dispose of make arrangements for
presently immediately

YORK God for His mercy! What a tide of woes
　　　　Comes rushing on this woeful land at once!
　　　　I know not what to do. I would to God,　　　　　　　　　100
　　　　So my untruth had not provoked him to it,
　　　　The king had cut off my head with my brother's.
　　　　What, are there no posts despatched for Ireland?
　　　　How shall we do for money for these wars?
　　　　Come, sister – cousin I would say, pray pardon me.　　105
　　　　Go, fellow, get thee home. Provide some carts
　　　　And bring away the armour that is there.
　　　　　　　　　　　　　　　　　[Exit Servingman]

　　　　Gentlemen, will you go muster men?
　　　　If I know how or which way to order these affairs
　　　　Thus disorderly thrust into my hands　　　　　　　　110
　　　　Never believe me. Both are my kinsmen.
　　　　T'one is my sovereign, whom both my oath
　　　　And duty bids defend; t'other again
　　　　Is my kinsman, whom the king hath wronged,
　　　　Whom conscience and my kindred bids to right.　　115
　　　　Well, somewhat we must do. Come, cousin.
　　　　I'll dispose of you. Gentlemen, go muster up your men
　　　　And meet me presently at Berkeley Castle.
　　　　I should to Plashy too,
　　　　But time will not permit. All is uneven　　　　　　　120
　　　　And everything is left at six and seven.
　　　　　　　　　　　　　　　Exeunt York and Queen

Bushy, Green and Bagot, the king's favourites, contemplate their own future.

---

1 What to do? (in groups of three)

To lose in politics could mean losing your head. All those close to the king are in great danger. Sit around a table to read lines 122–47. Listen carefully and make your replies pick up on the thoughts and fears of the other two. Can you see any difference in character or behaviour between Bushy, Green and Bagot?

2 Ladders of thought (in pairs)

One person reads lines 122–47 through slowly, while the other listens and decides what the key words are in each line (about two per line). You could highlight these words by repeating/echoing them. Do this several times until you have decided what the key words are. Write them down in the form of a ladder like this:

news . . . Ireland
none . . . returns
enemy . . . unpossible.

You may well choose different words to begin. Join with another pair and talk about what your ladders reveal of the thoughts of these men.

3 Disintegration (in groups of six)

Present a dumb show of the whole scene but rehearse it in a style that conveys the sense of things breaking up. Run it at speed in the manner of an early silent movie.

---

levy power proportionable
 to raise an army equal to
presages fears for the future

that's as York thrives that
 depends on York's success (in
 beating Bullingbrook)

BUSHY The wind sits fair for news to go for Ireland
But none returns. For us to levy power
Proportionable to the enemy is all unpossible.
GREEN Besides, our nearness to the king in love   125
Is near the hate of those love not the king.
BAGOT And that's the wavering commons, for their love
Lies in their purses, and whoso empties them
By so much fills their hearts with deadly hate.
BUSHY Wherein the king stands generally condemned.   130
BAGOT If judgement lie in them then so do we,
Because we ever have been near the king.
GREEN Well, I will for refuge straight to Bristow Castle.
The Earl of Wiltshire is already there.
BUSHY Thither will I with you, for little office   135
Will the hateful commons perform for us,
Except like curs to tear us all to pieces.
Will you go along with us?
BAGOT No, I will to Ireland to his majesty.
Farewell. If heart's presages be not vain   140
We three here part that ne'er shall meet again.
BUSHY That's as York thrives to beat back Bullingbrook.
GREEN Alas, poor duke! The task he undertakes
Is numbering sands and drinking oceans dry.
Where one on his side fights thousands will fly.   145
Farewell at once, for once, for all, and ever.
BUSHY Well, we may meet again.
BAGOT   I fear me never.   *Exeunt*

Bullingbrook, accompanied by Northumberland, makes his way through Gloucestershire towards Berkeley Castle.

1 Sincerity or flattery? (in groups of four)

As Richard's supporters flee for their lives, we see the cause of their panic. Northumberland has joined forces with Bullingbrook. But how genuine is the friendship?

Look at lines 1–20. One person is Bullingbrook. The others take a sentence or so each and speak to Bullingbrook:

a with genuine friendship
b in a very polite and formal manner
c very ingratiating and grovelling.

Ask Bullingbrook which approach seems most successful.

Eric Porter as Bullingbrook

2 The Earl of Northumberland

If you were Bullingbrook and Northumberland spoke lines 2–18 to you, how would you feel?

---

sugar a rare delicacy
Cotshall the Cotswolds
in Ross . . . by Ross . . .
wanting lacking
beguiled eased
tediousness and process the tedious progress

whencesoever from somewhere or other
dispersed the Household – a decisive act – the Royal Household ran the king's administrative system

ACT 2   SCENE 3
In Gloucestershire

Enter BULLINGBROOK *and* NORTHUMBERLAND

BULLINGBROOK How far is it, my lord, to Berkeley now?
NORTHUMBERLAND Believe me, noble lord,
    I am a stranger here in Gloucestershire.
    These high wild hills and rough uneven ways
    Draws out our miles and makes them wearisome. 5
    And yet your fair discourse hath been as sugar,
    Making the hard way sweet and delectable.
    But I bethink me what a weary way
    From Ravenspurgh to Cotshall will be found
    In Ross and Willoughby, wanting your company, 10
    Which I protest hath very much beguiled
    The tediousness and process of my travel.
    But theirs is sweetened with the hope to have
    The present benefit which I possess,
    And hope to joy is little less in joy 15
    Than hope enjoyed. By this the weary lords
    Shall make their way seem short as mine hath done
    By sight of what I have, your noble company.
BULLINGBROOK Of much less value is my company
    Than your good words. But who comes here? 20

Enter HARRY PERCY.

NORTHUMBERLAND It is my son, young Harry Percy,
    Sent from my brother Worcester whencesoever.
    Harry, how fares your uncle?
PERCY I had thought, my lord, to have learned his health of you.
NORTHUMBERLAND Why, is he not with the queen? 25
PERCY No, my good lord, he hath forsook the court,
    Broken his staff of office and dispersed
    The Household of the king.
NORTHUMBERLAND   What was his reason?
    He was not so resolved when last we spake together.

First Harry Percy and then Ross and Willoughby pledge their support for Bullingbrook in his attempt to claim his inheritance.

---

1 'Have you forgot the Duke of Herford, boy?'
(in groups of three)

One production, which made great use of the ceremony of kneeling in the opening scenes of this play, had these stage actions here:

Start of line 40: Northumberland (N) brings Percy downstage level with Bullingbrook (B)

Middle of line 40: N turns Percy to face Duke

End of line 40: pushes Percy to his knees

Start of line 45: B kneels right of Percy and takes his hands

Start of line 48: B lifts Percy to his feet

Start of line 50: B embraces Percy; middle of line: shakes P's hand

Start of line 57: Ross and Willoughby run on up to B and kneel.

Rehearse these moves and talk about why this production should want to echo the kneeling ceremonies of the opening scenes.

2 Glimpses into the future

An Elizabethan audience would probably have known that Bullingbrook's new allies (Northumberland, Percy and Worcester) would lead a rebellion against him some years later. One production hinted at this by having Percy burst in here and push Bullingbrook aside as he sat down to rest. What other ways might a production highlight the future threat to Bullingbrook of this young man?

The historical Percy (Hotspur) was two years older than Bullingbrook. Shakespeare probably made him much younger so that he could become the rival of Bullingbrook's son (Prince Hal) in the sequel play *Henry IV Part 1*.

---

desert worth, merit
gentle Percy noble Percy
stir activity
three hundred men Holinshed records that York had a 'puissant

power' but none of them would fight against Bullingbrook
I wot I assume, know
unfelt intangible, immaterial
evermore thank's . . . poor thanks are all that the poor can offer

PERCY Because your lordship was proclaimèd traitor.   30
   But he, my lord, is gone to Ravenspurgh
   To offer service to the Duke of Herford,
   And sent me over by Berkeley to discover
   What power the Duke of York had levied there,
   Then with directions to repair to Ravenspurgh.   35
NORTHUMBERLAND Have you forgot the Duke of Herford, boy?
PERCY No, my good lord, for that is not forgot
   Which ne'er I did remember. To my knowledge
   I never in my life did look on him.
NORTHUMBERLAND Then learn to know him now. This is the duke.   40
PERCY My gracious lord, I tender you my service,
   Such as it is, being tender, raw and young,
   Which elder days shall ripen and confirm
   To more approvèd service and desert.
BULLINGBROOK I thank thee, gentle Percy, and be sure   45
   I count myself in nothing else so happy
   As in a soul remembering my good friends,
   And as my fortune ripens with thy love
   It shall be still thy true love's recompense.
   My heart this covenant makes, my hand thus seals it.   50
NORTHUMBERLAND How far is it to Berkeley, and what stir
   Keeps good old York there with his men of war?
PERCY There stands the castle by yon tuft of trees,
   Manned with three hundred men as I have heard,
   And in it are the lords of York, Berkeley and Seymour,   55
   None else of name and noble estimate.

Enter ROSS *and* WILLOUGHBY.

NORTHUMBERLAND Here come the lords of Ross and Willoughby,
   Bloody with spurring, fiery red with haste.
BULLINGBROOK Welcome, my lords. I wot your love pursues
   A banished traitor. All my treasury   60
   Is yet but unfelt thanks, which, more enriched,
   Shall be your love and labour's recompense.
ROSS Your presence makes us rich, most noble lord.
WILLOUGHBY And far surmounts our labour to attain it.
BULLINGBROOK Evermore thank's the exchequer of the poor,   65
   Which till my infant fortune comes to years
   Stands for my bounty. But who comes here?

Bullingbrook faces the anger of his uncle, York.

---

1 Shows of ceremony (in pairs)

At this delicate moment in the shifting balance of power, every meeting, every greeting, every handshake is significant in signalling strength, weakness, support, opposition. Consider Bullingbrook's two meetings here:

a with Lord Berkeley, who comes with a message from York, Governor of England (lines 67–81)

b with his uncle, York (lines 82–90).

Rehearse both meetings, showing the differences between them. Think about the degrees of courtesy and respect (genuine or pretended) shown by the different men. Show your version to the rest of the class.

2 How angry is York? (in large groups)

Look at lines 86–104. As York confronted Richard, he now confronts Bullingbrook.

Split into two halves and stand in a line facing each other about six feet apart. Each group reads alternate sentences of York's speech. As your group speaks a sentence you must advance towards your opposite number and make them retreat. Then they in turn will advance towards you as they speak their sentence. How convincing do you find York's rebuke of his nephew?

---

raze take away, erase
pricks spurs
absent time time of absence (of the king)
ungracious wicked, sinful
profane blasphemous

anointed king many believed the anointing of the king at his coronation turned him into a sacred being. Who uses a similar phrase in 1.2?
palsy shaking sickness (often suffered by the old)

Enter BERKELEY.

NORTHUMBERLAND It is my lord of Berkeley, as I guess.
BERKELEY My lord of Herford, my message is to you.
BULLINGBROOK My lord, my answer is, to Lancaster,   70
    And I am come to seek that name in England,
    And I must find that title in your tongue
    Before I make reply to aught you say.
BERKELEY Mistake me not, my lord, 'tis not my meaning
    To raze one title of your honour out.   75
    To you, my lord, I come – what lord you will –
    From the most gracious regent of this land,
    The Duke of York, to know what pricks you on
    To take advantage of the absent time
    And fright our native peace with self-born arms?   80

Enter YORK.

BULLINGBROOK I shall not need transport my words by you.
    Here comes his grace in person. My noble uncle. [*Kneels.*]
YORK Show me thy humble heart and not thy knee,
    Whose duty is deceivable and false.
BULLINGBROOK My gracious uncle –   85
YORK Tut, tut! Grace me no grace, nor uncle me no uncle.
    I am no traitor's uncle, and that word grace
    In an ungracious mouth is but profane.
    Why have those banished and forbidden legs
    Dared once to touch a dust of England's ground?   90
    But then, more why? Why have they dared to march
    So many miles upon her peaceful bosom,
    Frighting her pale-faced villages with war
    And ostentation of despisèd arms?
    Comest thou because the anointed king is hence?   95
    Why, foolish boy, the king is left behind
    And in my loyal bosom lies his power.
    Were I but now lord of such hot youth
    As when brave Gaunt, thy father, and myself
    Rescued the Black Prince, that young Mars of men,   100
    From forth the ranks of many thousand French,
    Oh then how quickly should this arm of mine,
    Now prisoner to the palsy, chastise thee
    And minister correction to thy fault!

Bullingbrook defends his actions in returning to England.

---

1 A crucial speech (in groups of five)

Richard may have acted wrongly in seizing Gaunt's lands, but that does *not* make Bullingbrook's actions right. York commands the royal forces left in England. If Bullingbrook cannot win York over, the supporters of Richard will have a leader to rally round. If York sides with Bullingbrook, Richard is surely doomed.

Each person reads a section of lines 112–35, making Bullingbrook as brisk and confident as they can. Imagine that you are a lawyer in court, or are speaking in a debate. Which of Bullingbrook's arguments closely echoes York's very own arguments used against Richard in 2.1.187–208?

In one production, Bullingbrook put his arm around York and brought him downstage towards the audience. Find the line where you think that was done.

2 'Base men by his endowments are made great'

'High' images were used in Act 1 to describe Bullingbrook. Be alert from now on to 'base' images. 'Base men' are the lesser nobles to whom Richard gave Bullingbrook's confiscated lands ('endowments') as a reward for their services and loyalty (see also 2.1.241–2). What does Willoughby's remark (line 138) suggest is the real reason for his concern about Bullingbrook?

---

on what condition stands it? what law have I broken?
for Lancaster to assume the rights of Lancaster
indifferent impartial
perforce by force
unthrifts spendthrifts, wasters

chase them to the bay hunting image (as in 'brought to bay')
denied to sue my livery/letters patents (see 2.1.202–04)
distrained seized
challenge law demand my rights
of free descent by legal right

BULLINGBROOK My gracious uncle, let me know my fault.   105
    On what condition stands it and wherein?
YORK Even in condition of the worst degree,
    In gross rebellion and detested treason.
    Thou art a banished man, and here art come
    Before the expiration of thy time   110
    In braving arms against thy sovereign.
BULLINGBROOK As I was banished, I was banished Herford;
    But as I come, I come for Lancaster.
    And, noble uncle, I beseech your grace
    Look on my wrongs with an indifferent eye.   115
    You are my father, for methinks in you
    I see old Gaunt alive. Oh then, my father,
    Will you permit that I shall stand condemned
    A wandering vagabond, my rights and royalties
    Plucked from my arms perforce and given away   120
    To upstart unthrifts? Wherefore was I born?
    If that my cousin king be king in England
    It must be granted I am Duke of Lancaster.
    You have a son, Aumerle, my noble cousin.
    Had you first died and he been thus trod down   125
    He should have found his uncle Gaunt a father
    To rouse his wrongs and chase them to the bay.
    I am denied to sue my livery here,
    And yet my letters patents give me leave.
    My father's goods are all distrained and sold,   130
    And these and all are all amiss employed.
    What would you have me do? I am a subject,
    And I challenge law. Attorneys are denied me,
    And therefore personally I lay my claim
    To my inheritance of free descent.   135
NORTHUMBERLAND The noble duke hath been too much abused.
ROSS It stands your grace upon to do him right.
WILLOUGHBY Base men by his endowments are made great.

York decides to stay neutral in the conflict between Bullingbrook and Richard.

---

1 York's vacillation (in groups of three)

Historically, the evaporation of Richard's power was quite astounding, and this is one of a number of moments in the play which conveys that sense of disintegration. York's allegiances swing violently back and forth as he tries to resolve his dilemma.

Take a part each and read lines 139–70. Whenever York seems to change his mind, the other two must make him move to a new seat. Count the number of times this happens. Which line do you think marks the key moment in York's decision (or indecision)?

This is how one production staged the final exit:

Middle of line 158: York (Y) crosses to exit right. Way blocked by Bullingbrook (B)

End of line 161: B stops Y exiting left

Middle of line 167: all start to exit behind Y – Y returns to centre stage – everyone else returns to former positions

End of line 170: exeunt in order of precedence.

Stage this yourselves and see how even York's exit echoes his dilemma.

2 'The caterpillars of the commonwealth'

Think about the kind of damage caterpillars do in a garden. Is it apt to use this image to describe the king's 'favourites'? Be alert to echoes of caterpillars and gardens in later scenes.

---

kind manner, way
it may not be it must not be
issue outcome
mend prevent
attach arrest

neuter neutral (does it suggest anything else?)
Bristow Bristol
complices accomplices
nor friends . . . neither friends . . .

YORK My lords of England, let me tell you this:
    I have had feeling of my cousin's wrongs   140
    And laboured all I could to do him right.
    But in this kind to come, in braving arms,
    Be his own carver and cut out his way,
    To find out right with wrong? It may not be.
    And you that do abet him in this kind   145
    Cherish rebellion and are rebels all.
NORTHUMBERLAND The noble duke hath sworn his coming is
    But for his own, and for the right of that
    We all have strongly sworn to give him aid.
    And let him ne'er see joy that breaks that oath.   150
YORK Well, well. I see the issue of these arms.
    I cannot mend it, I must needs confess,
    Because my power is weak and all ill-left.
    But if I could, by Him that gave me life
    I would attach you all and make you stoop   155
    Unto the sovereign mercy of the king.
    But since I cannot, be it known unto you
    I do remain as neuter. So fare you well,
    Unless you please to enter in the castle
    And there repose you for this night.   160
BULLINGBROOK An offer, uncle, that we will accept.
    But we must win your grace to go with us
    To Bristow Castle, which they say is held
    By Bushy, Bagot and their complices,
    The caterpillars of the commonwealth,   165
    Which I have sworn to weed and pluck away.
YORK It may be I will go with you, but yet I'll pause,
    For I am loath to break our country's laws.
    Nor friends nor foes to me welcome you are.
    Things past redress are now with me past care.   170
                                     Exeunt

Richard's Welsh army disperses, believing the king to be dead.

---

1 Echoes of disaster (in groups of six)

Although the two characters in this scene play little part in the story, they create a particularly intense mood. We have watched Bullingbrook gain in strength. Now we see Richard's power ebbing away.

One RSC production had several characters on stage in this scene who echoed about seven words or phrases as the two named characters spoke them. Devise a group presentation of the Captain's words (lines 7–17) to show to the rest of the class using your own echoes.

2 Portents of doom

Halley's Comet

When Halley's Comet appeared in 1066 it 'foretold' the downfall of King Harold. List the signs and images in this scene which 'foretell' the downfall of Richard. One image will figure very powerfully in the next act. Which do you think it will be?

---

bay trees . . . are all withered a particularly bad omen, since bay leaves were a symbol of victory and immortality. Holinshed records this strange happening, but says it occurred in England, not Wales

enjoy possess
witnessing forecasting
wait upon serve, offer allegiance to
crossly contrary

ACT 2   SCENE 4
A camp in Wales

Enter Earl of SALISBURY and a Welsh CAPTAIN

CAPTAIN My lord of Salisbury, we have stayed ten days
  And hardly kept our countrymen together,
  And yet we hear no tidings from the king.
  Therefore we will disperse ourselves. Farewell.
SALISBURY Stay yet another day, thou trusty Welshman. 5
  The king reposeth all his confidence in thee.
CAPTAIN 'Tis thought the king is dead. We will not stay.
  The bay trees in our country are all withered
  And meteors fright the fixèd stars of heaven.
  The pale faced moon looks bloody on the earth, 10
  And lean looked prophets whisper fearful change.
  Rich men look sad and ruffians dance and leap,
  The one in fear to lose what they enjoy,
  The other to enjoy by rage and war.
  These signs forerun the death or fall of kings. 15
  Farewell. Our countrymen are gone and fled
  As well assured Richard their king is dead. *Exit*
SALISBURY Ah, Richard! With the eyes of heavy mind
  I see thy glory like a shooting star
  Fall to the base earth from the firmament. 20
  Thy sun sets weeping in the lowly west,
  Witnessing storms to come, woe and unrest.
  Thy friends are fled to wait upon thy foes
  And crossly to thy good all fortune goes. *Exit*

Looking back at Act 2

The shift in Richard's fortunes since the end of Act 1 has been quite dramatic. Taking advantage of the king's absence in Ireland, Bullingbrook and his supporters (especially Northumberland) have rapidly gained in strength. York is wavering in his support of the king and Richard's army is melting away.

1 Headlines

Write newspaper headlines for each of the scenes in Act 2. You could try it in a particular style: either popular tabloid or 'heavy'. Try to use some of Shakespeare's own words.

2 Communications

'The wind sits fair for news to go for Ireland
But none returns.'   Bushy (2.2.122–3)

Richard was unlucky with his communications at this crucial time. Imagine that the king and Bushy could communicate by fax machine. Write the messages that they would send each other. If you are really confident, compose them in 'Elizabethan' language. Better still, write them in blank verse (see page 202).

3 Interviewing King Richard

Several characters hostile to Richard have been allowed to comment in Act 2 on his policies and decisions, so allow the king a chance to defend himself. One person takes the role of King Richard. The others interview him for a television current affairs programme. Richard may find it helpful to read pages 191–5 before the interview. Either show the interview to the rest of the class, record it on tape, or write it up as a magazine article.

4 Perspectives

Rehearse a presentation of Act 2 Scene 2 lines 14–27 (in a group of four to six), using these RSC prompt copy notes. What particular perspective does this production seem to be taking?

Start of line 14: Bushy takes the queen's hand
Start of line 17: Bushy releases the queen's hand

Start of line 18: Bushy speaks out front
Middle of line 20: Bushy turns back to the queen
Middle of line 24: ladies and Bagot applaud.

5 First and last words

Read aloud the first four or five lines only of each scene. Do this several times and then talk together about the differences and/or similarities in the language of each opening. How far do these openings set a different mood for each scene?

Now say aloud several times the final line of each scene. Can you detect any change of mood from the opening lines of that scene? Do the final lines contrast in any way with the opening lines of the following scene?

6 Your thoughts on casting the play

You have already been asked to cast the role of the queen. Cast the roles of the other major characters:

- from the members of staff of your school or college
- from your class or year
- from film, television or the theatre.

Say why you think each might be suitable, but be ready to change your mind as you get further into the play!

7 Looking forward to Act 3

It is obvious from the events in Act 2 that Bullingbrook's banishment has not resolved the conflict between the two men, merely postponed it. In Act 3 their paths become inexorably closer, as Bullingbrook consolidates his strength and Richard returns from Ireland.

Although Richard's deposition and the symbolic transfer of the crown does not occur until Act 4, this act contains an equally significant scene, because Scene 3 at Flint Castle is the moment when actual power changes hands.

The final scene of Act 3, the garden scene, has been called 'the heart of the play'. Look for echoes of Gaunt's vision of his ideal England in it. This scene was also used as the inspiration for the stage set of the 1986 RSC production (see pages 185 and 189).

Bullingbrook condemns Bushy and Green, the king's favourites, to death.

---

1 A show trial? (in groups of three)

First read through the whole of this short scene. Each person then finds and reads out, as if they were in a court of law, one of the three major accusations that Bullingbrook makes against Bushy and Green. From the evidence in the play itself, which accusations are valid and which are unfounded? Talk about the manner in which Bushy and Green face death and compare Bullingbrook's manner of dispensing justice with Richard's in Act 1 Scenes 1 and 3.

The Price of Failure
(a contemporary drawing of the execution of the king's favourites)

---

urging emphasising
wash your blood . . . hands which New Testament character did exactly this?
lineaments features
clean completely
signories properties, estates

disparked my parks converted my hunting preserves to other uses
torn broken
coat coat of arms
razed out my imprese erased my heraldic crest

ACT 3 SCENE 1
Bristol In front of the castle

Enter BULLINGBROOK, YORK, NORTHUMBERLAND, ROSS, PERCY,
WILLOUGHBY, *with* BUSHY *and* GREEN *prisoners*

BULLINGBROOK Bring forth these men.
        Bushy and Green, I will not vex your souls,
        Since presently your souls must part your bodies,
        With too much urging your pernicious lives,
        For 'twere no charity. Yet to wash your blood   5
        From off my hands, here in the view of men
        I will unfold some causes of your deaths.
        You have misled a prince, a royal king,
        A happy gentleman in blood and lineaments
        By you unhappied and disfigured clean.   10
        You have in manner with your sinful hours
        Made a divorce betwixt his queen and him,
        Broke the possession of a royal bed
        And stained the beauty of a fair queen's cheeks
        With tears drawn from her eyes by your foul wrongs.   15
        Myself, a prince by fortune of my birth,
        Near to the king in blood and near in love
        Till you did make him misinterpret me,
        Have stooped my neck under your injuries
        And sighed my English breath in foreign clouds,   20
        Eating the bitter bread of banishment
        Whilst you have fed upon my signories,
        Disparked my parks and felled my forest woods,
        From my own windows torn my household coat,
        Razed out my imprese, leaving me no sign   25
        Save men's opinions and my living blood
        To show the world I am a gentleman.
        This and much more, much more than twice all this,
        Condemns you to the death. See them delivered over
        To execution and the hand of death.   30
BUSHY More welcome is the stroke of death to me
        Than Bullingbrook to England. Lords, farewell.
GREEN My comfort is that heaven will take our souls
        And plague injustice with the pains of hell.

*Bullingbrook moves to fight against Richard's Welsh army, unaware
that it has already dispersed. Richard lands in Wales, equally unaware of
what has happened.*

1 Contrast Richard and Bullingbrook
(in groups of twelve or more)

The Elizabethan stage was well-suited to the presentation of scenes
in quick succession, with the actors leaving the stage almost brushing
shoulders with those about to enter. Indeed, early editions of
Shakespeare's plays did not divide the script into scenes or acts at all.
Here we see the two major protagonists almost simultaneously and
can compare their qualities as leaders.

Half the group take Bullingbrook's exit (3.1.35–44). Talk about
how you think it should be staged and then rehearse it. The other half
take Richard's return from Ireland (3.2.1–22). Talk about how you
think it should be staged and then rehearse it.

Present the two pieces in sequence without a pause. Ask the
followers of each man how they feel about their leader.

2 'I weep for joy' (in pairs or groups of three)

If you recall the callous and unfeeling Richard who left for Ireland in
Act 2, be prepared for a surprise.

Take it in turns to read Richard's homecoming speech (lines
4–26). Talk together about your impressions of the king here,
particularly his feelings for the country he has been accused of
misgoverning. The 'internal stage direction' in line 23 shows the
reactions of Richard's companions. Are they your reactions, too?

---

intreated treated
at large in full
Glendower Welsh leader (one of
  the rebels in *Henry IV Part 1*)
complices accomplices

drums, flourish and colours
  usually signified the entrance of an
  army and the start of an important
  military scene. See what happens
  here
Barkloughly Harlech
brooks suits

BULLINGBROOK My Lord Northumberland, see them dispatched.   35
                    [Exeunt Northumberland and prisoners]
       Uncle, you say the queen is at your house.
       For God's sake fairly let her be intreated.
       Tell her I send to her my kind commends.
       Take special care my greetings be delivered.
YORK A gentleman of mine I have dispatched   40
       With letters of your love to her at large.
BULLINGBROOK Thanks, gentle uncle. Come, lords, away,
       To fight with Glendower and his complices.
       A while to work, and after holiday.
                                        Exeunt

ACT 3   SCENE 2
The coast of Wales

Drums, flourish and colours. Enter RICHARD, AUMERLE, CARLISLE
                 and soldiers

RICHARD Barkloughly Castle call they this at hand?
AUMERLE Yea, my lord. How brooks your grace the air
       After your late tossing on the breaking seas?
RICHARD Needs must I like it well. I weep for joy
       To stand upon my kingdom once again.   5
       Dear earth, I do salute thee with my hand,
       Though rebels wound thee with their horses' hooves.
       As a long-parted mother with her child
       Plays fondly with her tears and smiles in meeting,
       So weeping, smiling, greet I thee, my earth,   10
       And do thee favours with my royal hands.
       Feed not thy sovereign's foe, my gentle earth,
       Nor with thy sweets comfort his ravenous sense
       But let thy spiders that suck up thy venom
       And heavy-gaited toads lie in their way,   15
       Doing annoyance to the treacherous feet
       Which with usurping steps do trample thee.
       Yield stinging nettles to mine enemies,
       And when they from thy bosom pluck a flower
       Guard it, I pray thee, with a lurking adder   20
       Whose double tongue may with a mortal touch
       Throw death upon thy sovereign's enemies.

Carlisle and Aumerle urge Richard to make practical plans to deal with the rebellion but the king seems confident that Bullingbrook will fail.

An account of the young Richard at his coronation:

'As he lay on the cloth of gold cushions and felt his head and body anointed with the oil through the unlaced gaps in his clothing, he felt flow from the Archbishop of Canterbury's fingers the Grace of God, changing and making him more than a man, a *persona mixta*. For many years afterwards he was to refer to the signs of the cross they made on his body, on his head, in the palms of his hands, on his breast, between his shoulders and on his arms as an indication that he felt he had been marked unalterably and forever by God.'

M. L. Bruce *The Usurper King*

1 Richard the sun king (in pairs)

The rising sun was Richard's personal emblem. Read lines 36–62, taking a sentence each. Why is Richard so confident? (see also pages 191 and 198–9 on Richard's concept of kingship)

my senseless conjuration my appeal to the unresponsive earth
the means . . . redress i.e. 'God helps those who help themselves'
security over-confidence

discomfortable disheartening
antipodes opposite side of the earth
pressed conscripted
shrewd harmful

Mock not my senseless conjuration, lords.
This earth shall have a feeling and these stones
Prove armèd soldiers ere her native king   25
Shall falter under foul rebellion's arms.
CARLISLE Fear not, my lord. That power that made you king
Hath power to keep you king in spite of all.
The means that heavens yield must be embraced
And not neglected. Else heaven would   30
And we will not. Heavens offer, we refuse
The proffered means of succour and redress.
AUMERLE He means, my lord, that we are too remiss
Whilst Bullingbrook through our security
Grows strong and great in substance and in power.   35
RICHARD Discomfortable cousin, knowest thou not
That when the searching eye of heaven is hid
Behind the globe and lights the lower world
Then thieves and robbers range abroad unseen
In murders and in outrage boldly here.   40
But when from under this terrestrial ball
He fires the proud tops of the eastern pines
And darts his light through every guilty hole
Then murders, treasons and detested sins,
The cloak of night being plucked from off their backs,   45
Stand bare and naked, trembling at themselves?
So when this thief, this traitor, Bullingbrook,
Who all this while hath revelled in the night
Whilst we were wandering with the antipodes
Shall see us rising in our throne the east   50
His treasons will sit blushing in his face,
Not able to endure the sight of day,
But self-affrighted tremble at his sin.
Not all the water in the rough rude sea
Can wash the balm off from an anointed king.   55
The breath of worldly men cannot depose
The deputy elected by the Lord.
For every man that Bullingbrook hath pressed
To lift shrewd steel against our golden crown
God for His Richard hath in heavenly pay   60
A glorious angel. Then if angels fight
Weak men must fall, for heaven still guards the right.

Richard is dismayed by Salisbury's news of the defection of his Welsh army, but tries to rally his spirits.

---

1 Images of time (in groups of four to six)

As one person reads Salisbury's speech (lines 64–74), the rest echo all the 'time' words that occur.

Richard's timing at this crucial moment was not good. Once the king had embarked for Ireland, favourable winds carried Bullingbrook with ease to Ravenspurgh. Then, when Bullingbrook was safely landed, the weather changed and made it impossible for Richard to get quickly back from Ireland.

Talk together about other ways in which time has featured in the play so far.

2 Hope, despair, recovery, resignation (in groups of six)

As if to emphasise Richard's helplessness in the face of events, messengers arrive with disturbing news.

Three of you be Salisbury, Aumerle and Scroope. The rest take Richard's role and read his words in unison. Start this section, standing next to a chair. As lines 63–103 are spoken and reacted to, the Richards decide whether they should sit, stand, stand on the chair or collapse to the floor. In other words, they rise or fall physically to match Richard's rise and fall in confidence. Rising and falling images will become very insistent as the crucial transfer of power draws near.

---

set a blot cast a stain, or slur
care-tuned tuned to the note of sorrow
deliver him bring or tell him

'twas my care my responsibility Richard has always been very sensitive to words (see 1.1.25). What prompts him to use this phrase?

Enter SALISBURY.

Welcome, my lord. How far off lies your power?
SALISBURY Nor near nor farther off, my gracious lord,
Than this weak arm. Discomfort guides my tongue   65
And bids me speak of nothing but despair.
One day too late, I fear me, noble lord,
Hath clouded all thy happy days on earth.
Oh call back yesterday, bid time return
And thou shalt have twelve thousand fighting men.   70
Today, today, unhappy day too late
O'erthrows thy joys, friends, fortune and thy state,
For all the Welshmen, hearing thou wert dead,
Are gone to Bullingbrook, dispersed and fled.
AUMERLE Comfort, my liege. Why looks your grace so pale?   75
RICHARD But now the blood of twenty thousand men
Did triumph in my face, and they are fled,
And till so much blood thither come again
Have I not reason to look pale and dead?
All souls that will be safe fly from my side,   80
For time hath set a blot upon my pride.
AUMERLE Comfort, my liege. Remember who you are.
RICHARD I had forgot myself. Am I not king?
Awake, thou coward! Majesty, thou sleepest.
Is not the king's name twenty thousand names?   85
Arm, arm, my name! A puny subject strikes
At thy great glory. Look not to the ground.
Ye favourites of a king, are we not high?
High be our thoughts. I know my uncle York
Hath power enough to serve our turn. But who comes
here?   90

Enter SCROOPE.

SCROOPE More health and happiness betide my liege
Than can my care-tuned tongue deliver him.
RICHARD My ear is open and my heart prepared.
The worst is worldly loss thou canst unfold.
Say, is my kingdom lost? Why, 'twas my care   95
And what loss is it to be rid of care?

Scroope tells of Bullingbrook's gathering strength and popular support throughout the country. Richard is angry at the apparent defection of Bushy, Green and Bagot.

1 'Too well, too well thou tell'st a tale so ill'
(in groups of four to six)

Do not forget the dramatic impact of the messenger, particularly when events are rapidly changing.

Read Scroope's news (lines 104–20), changing readers at each punctuation mark (so that each person reads a sense unit). Read it through several times. Many lines 'run on' or 'overflow' from the end of one line into the next and the speech finishes with a final couplet (lines 119–20). How does all this help Scroope convey to Richard and to us the news that the whole kingdom seems to have turned against its king? (see pages 202–03 for details on blank verse structure)

2 Recurring images

a Earth, air, fire and water
These are the four elements (see page 200). Richard likens himself to the sun (3.2.36–53). To which element does Scroope liken Bullingbrook and why?

b Christ betrayed
Find the line where Richard likens himself to Christ. Be alert to how this image is developed in later scenes.

c Sweet and sour
Read lines 135–6. What connection does this image have with the fortunes of the two major characters?

3 Richard's anger (in small groups)

Richard's famous anger flares again. Take a sentence each from lines 129–34 and hurl it as loudly as you can at the rest of the group. Richard's anger does not seem to bother Scroope, however!

---

beadsmen old men paid to say prayers for their benefactors ('beads' are prayers on a rosary)
double-fatal yew how does yew kill in two ways?
distaff stick used for spinning wool

bills halberds, old-fashioned weapons used by the parish guard
Bagot did not in fact die. We see him very much alive in Act 4
measure pass through
his property its distinctive quality

Strives Bullingbrook to be as great as we,
Greater he shall not be. If he serve God
We'll serve Him too, and be his fellow so.
Revolt our subjects? That we cannot mend.   100
They break their faith to God as well as us.
Cry woe, destruction, ruin and decay.
The worst is death, and death will have his day.

SCROOPE Glad am I that your highness is so armed
To bear the tidings of calamity.   105
Like an unseasonable stormy day
Which makes the silver rivers drown their shores
As if the world were all dissolved to tears,
So high above his limits swells the rage
Of Bullingbrook, covering your fearful land   110
With hard bright steel and hearts harder than steel.
Whitebeards have armed their thin and hairless scalps
Against thy majesty, boys with women's voices
Strive to speak big, and clap their female joints
In stiff unwieldy arms against thy crown.   115
Thy very beadsmen learn to bend their bows
Of double-fatal yew against thy state.
Yea, distaff women manage rusty bills
Against thy seat. Both young and old rebel
And all goes worse than I have power to tell.   120

RICHARD Too well, too well thou tell'st a tale so ill.
Where is the Earl of Wiltshire, where is Bagot,
What is become of Bushy, where is Green,
That they have let the dangerous enemy
Measure our confines with such peaceful steps?   125
If we prevail their heads shall pay for it.
I warrant they have made peace with Bullingbrook.

SCROOPE Peace have they made with him indeed, my lord.

RICHARD Oh villains, vipers, damned without redemption!
Dogs, easily won to fawn on any man!   130
Snakes in my heart blood warmed, that sting my heart!
Three Judases, each one thrice worse than Judas!
Would they make peace? Terrible hell
Make war upon their spotted souls for this!

SCROOPE Sweet love I see, changing his property,   135
Turns to the sourest and most deadly hate.

97

On learning of the deaths of Bushy, Green and the Earl of Wiltshire, Richard wishes to hear no more. His thoughts now dwell on deeper things.

---

1 'How can you say to me I am a king?' (in groups of four)

Close up of the statue of Henry V placing on his own head the same crown that his father, Henry Bullingbrook, had seized from Richard II.

a A new wisdom

Events are forcing Richard to a wisdom that power and prosperity could never teach him. Speak lines 144–77 to each other handing on to the next speaker at every punctuation mark. Talk about the nature of Richard's new-found wisdom.

b Hollowness

Three images express a sense of outer coverings barely concealing an inner emptiness (lines 152–4, 160–03, 169–70). Read these lines, close your eyes and imagine the pictures. Share your mind pictures or draw them.

c Key words

Make a 'word ladder' of the key words (see page 72 for an example of how to do this). Talk about Richard's preoccupations here.

---

model mound, mould, outline
paste pastry
antic jester, grotesque figure (there were many medieval pictures of death as a skeleton grinning at the preoccupations of men with wealth and power)

kill with looks exercise the power of the king's gaze (see page 56)
cover your heads removing hats was a gesture of respect in the presence of a king

Again uncurse their souls. Their peace is made
With heads and not with hands. Those whom you curse
Have felt the worst of death's destroying wound
And lie full low, graved in the hollow ground.   140
AUMERLE Is Bushy, Green, and the Earl of Wiltshire dead?
SCROOPE Ay, all of them at Bristow lost their heads.
AUMERLE Where is the duke my father with his power?
RICHARD No matter where. Of comfort no man speak.
Let's talk of graves, of worms and epitaphs,   145
Make dust our paper and with rainy eyes
Write sorrow on the bosom of the earth.
Let's choose executors and talk of wills.
And yet not so, for what can we bequeath
Save our deposèd bodies to the ground?   150
Our lands, our lives and all are Bullingbrook's,
And nothing can we call our own but death,
And that small model of the barren earth
Which serves as paste and cover to our bones.
For God's sake let us sit upon the ground   155
And tell sad stories of the death of kings,
How some have been deposed, some slain in war,
Some haunted by the ghosts they have deposed,
Some poisoned by their wives, some sleeping killed,
All murdered. For within the hollow crown   160
That rounds the mortal temples of a king
Keeps Death his court, and there the antic sits
Scoffing his state and grinning at his pomp,
Allowing him a breath, a little scene
To monarchise, be feared and kill with looks,   165
Infusing him with self and vain conceit
As if this flesh which walls about our life
Were brass impregnable, and humoured thus
Comes at the last and with a little pin
Bores through his castle wall and farewell king!   170
Cover your heads, and mock not flesh and blood
With solemn reverence. Throw away respect,
Tradition, form and ceremonious duty,
For you have but mistook me all this while.
I live with bread like you, feel want,   175
Taste grief, need friends. Subjected thus,
How can you say to me I am a king?

Aumerle and Carlisle attempt once more to rally the spirits of the king.
But Scroope has yet more bad news to tell.

1 Feel the desperation (in groups of three)

Two of you be Carlisle and Aumerle and read lines 178–87. Try to rouse your king's spirits. Richard, however, must make it as difficult as he can by his movements and reactions (for example, he might sit with his hands over his ears). Swap roles and try it again.

2 Facing up to the crisis (in groups of four)

Take a part each. Sit or stand facing each other. Read this page through twice, each time attempting to present your character's attitude to the events around him. Then ask each other how you feel at this moment.

3 Swings of mood (individually or in groups of eight or more)

Choose eight to ten quotes from the whole scene which best illustrate Richard's fluctuating moods and devise a way of presenting them.

- If you are on your own, either a chart, diagram or a graph.
  Compare your version with someone else's analysis and argue over the differences.
- If you are working as a group, think of a more physically active way
  – perhaps a speaking tableau or sequence of 'film clips'.

presently immediately
oppresseth undermines
fear and be slain if you are afraid
  you will certainly be killed
where fearing . . . whereas
  fearing . . .

doom judgement
ague fever
upon his party on his side
of that sweet way from that
to ear the land to plough the land

CARLISLE My lord, wise men ne'er sit and wail their woes,
　　　　　But presently prevent the ways to wail.
　　　　　To fear the foe, since fear oppresseth strength,　　　180
　　　　　Gives, in your weakness, strength unto your foe,
　　　　　And so your follies fight against your self.
　　　　　Fear and be slain. No worse can come to fight,
　　　　　And fight and die is death destroying death
　　　　　Where fearing dying pays death servile breath.　　　185
AUMERLE My father hath a power. Enquire of him
　　　　　And learn to make a body of a limb.
RICHARD Thou chid'st me well. Proud Bullingbrook, I come
　　　　　To change blows with thee for our day of doom.
　　　　　This ague fit of fear is overblown,　　　190
　　　　　An easy task it is to win our own.
　　　　　Say, Scroope, where lies our uncle with his power?
　　　　　Speak sweetly, man, although thy looks be sour.
SCROOPE Men judge by the complexion of the sky
　　　　　The state and inclination of the day;　　　195
　　　　　So may you by my dull and heavy eye.
　　　　　My tongue hath but a heavier tale to say.
　　　　　I play the torturer by small and small
　　　　　To lengthen out the worst that must be spoken.
　　　　　Your uncle York is joined with Bullingbrook　　　200
　　　　　And all your northern castles yielded up,
　　　　　And all your southern gentlemen in arms
　　　　　Upon his party.
RICHARD　　　　　　Thou hast said enough.
　　　　　[To Aumerle] Beshrew thee, cousin, which didst lead me
　　　　　　　forth
　　　　　Of that sweet way I was in to despair.　　　205
　　　　　What say you now? What comfort have we now?
　　　　　By heaven I'll hate him everlastingly
　　　　　That bids me be of comfort any more.
　　　　　Go to Flint Castle, there I'll pine away.
　　　　　A king, woe's slave, shall kingly woe obey.　　　210
　　　　　That power I have, discharge, and let them go
　　　　　To ear the land that hath some hope to grow,
　　　　　For I have none. Let no man speak again
　　　　　To alter this, for counsel is but vain.

Bullingbrook and his supporters approach Flint Castle, where, unknown to them, King Richard has taken refuge.

---

1 The falling king

Read Richard's final words (lines 215–18). What, significantly, has happened to the sun image so prominent earlier in this scene?

2 The rising duke (in groups of three)

As the despairing Richard discharges the remains of his army, we see Bullingbrook moving swiftly to close in on the king. Bullingbrook is very much concerned with military matters (what does the opening line of the scene suggest he might have in his hand?). Things seem to be going as planned, but there are tensions, which come to the surface with York's rebuke to Northumberland.

Take a part each and read lines 1–19 several times. Try to convey the tensions between York and the other two. Look at how they take up each other's words (head, heads, brief, takes, mistakes) and emphasise that in your reading. Try different ways of reacting to York's rebukes (for example, genuinely apologetic, polite but unrepentant, cynical, contemptuous, amused).

Afterwards, quickly write down your thoughts at that moment about the other two men and about what is happening. Then exchange your thoughts with the others. What seems to be the cause of all the tensions?

---

intelligence information
beseem be fitting (for)
to shorten . . . length (as) to shorten by taking off your head for omitting his 'head' or title. 'Taking the head' could also mean 'acting impetuously'

mistake not . . . lest you
mistake can mean either 'do not misunderstand' or 'do not mis-take (i.e. take unlawfully)'. Which meaning does each man use?

AUMERLE My liege, one word.
RICHARD   He does me double wrong   215
          That wounds me with the flatteries of his tongue.
          Discharge my followers, let them hence away
          From Richard's night to Bullingbrook's fair day.

                                                    Exeunt

ACT 3   SCENE 3
Wales   In front of Flint Castle

Enter with drum and colours BULLINGBROOK, YORK,
NORTHUMBERLAND, *attendants*

BULLINGBROOK So that by this intelligence we learn
          The Welshmen are dispersed, and Salisbury
          Is gone to meet the king, who lately landed
          With some few private friends upon this coast.
NORTHUMBERLAND The news is very fair and good, my lord.   5
          Richard not far from hence hath hid his head.
YORK It would beseem the Lord Northumberland
          To say King Richard. Alack the heavy day
          When such a sacred king should hide his head.
NORTHUMBERLAND Your grace mistakes. Only to be brief   10
          Left I his title out.
YORK   The time hath been,
          Would you have been so brief with him he would
          Have been so brief with you to shorten you,
          For taking so the head, your whole head's length.
BULLINGBROOK Mistake not, uncle, further than you should.   15
YORK Take not, good cousin, further than you should,
          Lest you mistake. The heavens are o'er our heads.
BULLINGBROOK I know it, uncle, and oppose not myself
          Against their will. But who comes here?

Bullingbrook sends Northumberland to offer his allegiance to King Richard.

1 Another vital political speech (in groups of four)

The confrontation between king and duke is very close. Now more than ever must Bullingbrook be careful. He swore an oath at Doncaster (2.3.147–8) that he came only for his inheritance. Many nobles present might be suspicious and unsupportive if he made additional claims. Taking a sentence each, read lines 31–53. Decide how successfully Bullingbrook maintains the balance between impressing and reassuring his own aristocratic supporters.

2 Bullingbrook's surprise

Read the historical 'facts' as recorded in Holinshed (page 195). How do the changes Shakespeare has made to the events at Flint Castle affect your judgement of the part played by Bullingbrook and Northumberland in Richard's downfall?

3 'Oh, belike it is the Bishop of Carlisle' (in groups of three)

One reviewer of the RSC's 1980 production considered this to be the best delivered line in the play! Read lines 20–30. Take it in turns to be Northumberland while the others speak the parts of Percy and Bullingbrook. See how well you can deliver line 30.

---

parle truce
his ruined ears the ruined ears, or ramparts, of the castle (in Elizabethan grammar, 'his' could refer to inanimate things)

summer's dust historically it was August 1399
tottered tattered, ruined
appointments military equipment

Enter PERCY.

Welcome, Harry. What, will not this castle yield?   20
PERCY The castle royally is manned, my lord,
          Against thy entrance.
BULLINGBROOK Royally? Why, it contains no king.
PERCY Yes, my good lord.
          It doth contain a king. King Richard lies   25
          Within the limits of yon lime and stone,
          And with him are the Lord Aumerle, Lord Salisbury,
          Sir Stephen Scroope, besides a clergyman
          Of holy reverence; who, I cannot learn.
NORTHUMBERLAND Oh, belike it is the Bishop of Carlisle.   30
BULLINGBROOK Noble lord,
          Go to the rude ribs of that ancient castle.
          Through brazen trumpet send the breath of parle
          Into his ruined ears, and thus deliver:
          Henry Bullingbrook   35
          On both his knees doth kiss King Richard's hand
          And sends allegiance and true faith of heart
          To his most royal person; hither come
          Even at his feet to lay my arms and power,
          Provided that my banishment repealed   40
          And lands restored again be freely granted.
          If not I'll use the advantage of my power
          And lay the summer's dust with showers of blood
          Rained from the wounds of slaughtered Englishmen,
          The which how far off from the mind of Bullingbrook   45
          It is such crimson tempest should bedrench
          The fresh green lap of fair King Richard's land
          My stooping duty tenderly shall show.
          Go, signify as much while here we march
          Upon the grassy carpet of this plain.   50
          Let's march without the noise of threatening drum,
          That from this castle's tottered battlements
          Our fair appointments may be well perused.

Richard appears on the battlements of Flint Castle to answer Northumberland's call to talk. Bullingbrook and his followers observe from a distance.

1 Images of fire and water (in groups of four to six)

Bullingbrook senses the importance of this meeting. Two of you read lines 54–71. The rest repeat or echo any words connected with the elements of fire and water. Why should they occur here?

Name the characters in this reconstruction of an Elizabethan performance and decide which line is being spoken at this point.

parle without and answer within trumpet-calls for a parley (talk), first on stage and then backstage
occident west
lightens forth sends forth as lightning

awful duty duty of showing respect (how has Northumberland failed to show respect here?)
gripe grasp
all as . . . souls everyone has sinned like yourselves
vassal subject

Methinks King Richard and myself should meet
With no less terror than the elements   55
Of fire and water when their thundering shock
At meeting tears the cloudy cheeks of heaven.
Be he the fire, I'll be the yielding water.
The rage be his, whilst on the earth I rain
My waters; on the earth and not on him.   60
March on, and mark King Richard how he looks.

Parle without, and answer within. Then a flourish. Enter on the walls
RICHARD, CARLISLE, AUMERLE, SCROOPE, SALISBURY.

See, see, King Richard doth himself appear
As doth the blushing discontented sun
From out the fiery portal of the east
When he perceives the envious clouds are bent   65
To dim his glory and to stain the track
Of his bright passage to the occident.
YORK Yet looks he like a king. Behold, his eye,
As bright as is the eagle's, lightens forth
Controlling majesty. Alack, alack for woe   70
That any harm should stain so fair a show.
RICHARD [*To Northumberland*]
We are amazed, and thus long have we stood
To watch the fearful bending of thy knee
Because we thought ourself thy lawful king.
And if we be, how dare thy joints forget   75
To pay their awful duty to our presence?
If we be not, show us the hand of God
That hath dismissed us from our stewardship,
For well we know no hand of blood and bone
Can gripe the sacred handle of our sceptre,   80
Unless he do profane, steal or usurp.
And though you think that all as you have done
Have torn their souls by turning them from us
And we are barren and bereft of friends
Yet know: my master, God omnipotent,   85
Is mustering in his clouds on our behalf
Armies of pestilence, and they shall strike
Your children yet unborn and unbegot
That lift your vassal hands against my head
And threat the glory of my precious crown.   90

Northumberland assures Richard that Bullingbrook is only coming for his inheritance. The king assures Northumberland that Bullingbrook's demands will be met in full.

1 'Showers of blood' (in groups of four)

Two of you take it in turns to read Richard's vision of what England will be like if Bullingbrook takes the crown (lines 91–100). The other two listen and try to picture the scene that Richard paints. Describe your pictures to each other.

Now reverse roles and do the same with Bullingbrook's description of what England will be like if Richard does not agree to his demands (lines 42–8). How ominous do you find these two pictures?

2 Do you believe them? (in pairs)

Richard has already said that Bullingbrook wants the crown. Northumberland here assures Richard that this is not so.

Read lines 101–26 to each other, one as Northumberland, one as Richard. Pause every two lines or so to allow your partner to comment in role on what you have just said. Talk about how far you feel able to believe each other.

3 Images of blood

Compare the use Northumberland makes of blood images (lines 103–10) in reply to Richard's blood images (lines 75–81 and lines 93–100). Why might Northumberland do this?

---

testament a will (bequeathing a bloody war)
ere before
crown(s) can you see the two meanings in Richard's grim pun?
pastor priest, shepherd

civil as in 'civil war'
uncivil barbarous
lineal royalties hereditary rights
enfranchisement freedom from banishment (see 3.3.133–6)
barbèd protected by armour

Tell Bullingbrook, for yon methinks he stands,
That every stride he makes upon my land
Is dangerous treason. He is come to ope
The purple testament of bleeding war,
But ere the crown he looks for live in peace   95
Ten thousand bloody crowns of mothers' sons
Shall ill become the flower of England's face,
Change the complexion of her maid-pale peace
To scarlet indignation and bedew
Her pastor's grass with faithful English blood.   100
NORTHUMBERLAND The King of Heaven forbid our lord the king
Should so with civil and uncivil arms
Be rushed upon! Thy thrice noble cousin,
Harry Bullingbrook, doth humbly kiss thy hand
And by the honourable tomb he swears,   105
That stands upon your royal grandsire's bones,
And by the royalties of both your bloods,
Currents that spring from one most gracious head,
And by the buried hand of warlike Gaunt,
And by the worth and honour of himself,   110
Comprising all that may be sworn or said,
His coming hither hath no further scope
Than for his lineal royalties, and to beg
Enfranchisement immediate on his knees,
Which on thy royal party granted once   115
His glittering arms he will commend to rust,
His barbèd steeds to stables and his heart
To faithful service of your majesty.
This swears he as he is a prince and just,
And as I am a gentleman I credit him.   120
RICHARD Northumberland, say thus the king returns:
His noble cousin is right welcome hither,
And all the number of his fair demands
Shall be accomplished without contradiction.
With all the gracious utterance thou hast   125
Speak to his gentle hearing kind commends.

Northumberland conveys Richard's acceptance of the demands to Bullingbrook. Richard waits for Northumberland to return.

---

1 'We do debase ourselves' (in pairs)

Whatever else Richard may lack, he does not lack perception. This remark to Aumerle (line 127) seems to suggest that the king fears the worst may be about to happen – the loss of his titles, lands and even his life.

Regard Richard's speech (lines 143–75) as being in three parts:

a Richard speaks to himself (to others?) (lines 143–59)
b Richard speaks to Aumerle (lines 160–71).
c Richard speaks to Northumberland who has returned from Bullingbrook (lines 172–5).

Take turns to read these sections and talk about Richard's changes of thought. In one production, Richard delivered the line 'What must the king do now?' in a panicky gabble. How do you think the line is best delivered?

Next, try to see how the two states (Richard's present regal state and his future 'unkinged' state) are set against each other as he speaks. Read lines 143–54 taking a half-line each and handing over at the caesura (the mid-line pause), dividing each line where you feel the antithesis (contrast) is.

Finally, look at the words Richard speaks to Aumerle (lines 160–71). Read them to each other and then draw a cartoon picture of the two 'tears' images that Richard uses. An elaborate or fanciful image is termed a 'conceit'. Do your drawings suggest that these two images might be 'conceits'? Notice that Richard remarks on Aumerle's tears, then later remarks on his laughter. What kind of tears and what kind of laughter?

---

sooth appeasement, flattery
set of beads a rosary
gay apparel fine clothes (Richard was famous for this extravagance)
almsman man who receives charity
figured embossed, ornamented

palmer a pilgrim who has visited the Holy Land. Richard, like Bullingbrook (1.3.263), thinks of being a pilgrim
trade traffic

[*To Aumerle*] We do debase ourselves, cousin, do we not,
To look so poorly and to speak so fair?
Shall we call back Northumberland and send
Defiance to the traitor and so die?   130
AUMERLE No, good my lord. Let's fight with gentle words,
Till time lend friends, and friends their helpful swords.
RICHARD Oh God, oh God, that e'er this tongue of mine
That laid the sentence of dread banishment
On yon proud man should take it off again   135
With words of sooth! Oh that I were as great
As is my grief, or lesser than my name,
Or that I could forget what I have been,
Or not remember what I must be now!
Swell'st thou, proud heart? I'll give thee scope to beat,   140
Since foes have scope to beat both thee and me.
AUMERLE Northumberland comes back from Bullingbrook.
RICHARD What must the king do now? Must he submit?
The king shall do it. Must he be deposed?
The king shall be contented. Must he lose   145
The name of king? A God's name let it go.
I'll give my jewels for a set of beads,
My gorgeous palace for a hermitage,
My gay apparel for an almsman's gown,
My figured goblets for a dish of wood,   150
My sceptre for a palmer's walking staff,
My subjects for a pair of carvèd saints,
And my large kingdom for a little grave,
A little, little grave, an obscure grave.
Or I'll be buried in the king's highway,   155
Some way of common trade, where subjects' feet
May hourly trample on their sovereign's head;
For on my heart they tread now whilst I live,
And buried once, why not upon my head?

Richard descends to the lower court at Bullingbrook's request.

---

1 'May it please you to come down?'
(in groups of six to eight)

Northumberland's apparently polite request is full of menace. No king would descend to meet one of his subjects. The subject would be required to come up to him.

This symbolic falling is felt above all in lines 178–83. In the 1986 RSC production, as Richard said these words, the central tower on which he stood actually spiralled to the ground. Devise a way of presenting these lines, involving everyone in the group. Share out the lines, use echoes, repetitions or any other techniques that you think will create a verbal fall to match Richard's physical and political fall.

2 'Like glistering Phaëton' (in groups of four)

In the Greek legend, Phaëton was the son of Apollo, who drove the fiery sun chariot across the sky each day. Phaëton took his father's sun chariot but was unable to control the horses and drove the sun too near the earth. To save the world from destruction, Zeus struck him with a thunderbolt.

Read lines 178–83. Talk together about the parallels between Richard and Phaëton. Then imagine you are a political cartoonist. You overhear Richard speak lines 178–83 and decide to draw a cartoon for tomorrow's newspaper commenting on Richard's fall and showing him driving a sun chariot. Who or what would be the horses, the chariot, the sun, and Apollo? If your artistic skills are good enough, draw the cartoon.

---

lodge flatten
play the wantons amuse ourselves
fretted worn away
you make a leg . . . says aye you bow and Bullingbrook will do as you ask

base court outer or lower court (see the effect the word 'base' has on Richard)
wanting the manage unable to control
jades vicious horses
fondly foolishly

Aumerle, thou weep'st, my tender-hearted cousin.   160
We'll make foul weather with despisèd tears:
Our sighs and they shall lodge the summer corn
And make a dearth in this revolting land.
Or shall we play the wantons with our woes
And make some pretty match with shedding tears,   165
As thus to drop them still upon one place
Till they have fretted us a pair of graves
Within the earth, and therein laid? There lies
Two kinsmen digged their graves with weeping eyes.
Would not this ill do well? Well, well, I see   170
I talk but idly and you laugh at me.
Most mighty prince, my Lord Northumberland,
What says King Bullingbrook? Will his majesty
Give Richard leave to live till Richard die?
You make a leg and Bullingbrook says ay.   175

NORTHUMBERLAND My lord, in the base court he doth attend
   To speak with you. May it please you to come down?

RICHARD Down, down I come, like glistering Phaëton,
   Wanting the manage of unruly jades.
   In the base court? Base court where kings grow base   180
   To come at traitors' calls and do them grace!
   In the base court come down. Down court, down king,
   For night owls shriek where mounting larks should sing.

                              [*Richard descends*]

BULLINGBROOK What says his majesty?

NORTHUMBERLAND   Sorrow and grief of heart
   Makes him speak fondly like a frantic man.   185

Despite the rebels' show of respect, Richard is convinced that he is entirely in their power. Bullingbrook says that Richard is to go with him to London.

1 Royal splendour

Decide which line from Scene 3 is being spoken at this moment. Why should Richard choose to wear such a spectacular golden costume?

---

fair duty honourable respect, ceremonial kneeling
me rather had I had rather
thus high where does Richard point as he says this?

redoubted dreaded (does he mean it?)
want their remedies lack the ability to do anything about it

[*Enter Richard below.*]

  Yet he is come.
BULLINGBROOK Stand all apart
  And show fair duty to his majesty.
      He kneels down.
  My gracious lord.
RICHARD Fair cousin, you debase your princely knee
  To make the base earth proud with kissing it.   190
  Me rather had my heart might feel your love
  Than my unpleased eye see your courtesy.
  Up, cousin, up. Your heart is up, I know,
  Thus high at least, although your knee be low.
BULLINGBROOK My gracious lord, I come but for mine own. 195
RICHARD Your own is yours and I am yours and all.
BULLINGBROOK So far be mine, my most redoubted lord,
  As my true service shall deserve your love.
RICHARD Well you deserve. They well deserve to have
  That know the strong'st and surest way to get.   200
  Uncle, give me your hands. Nay, dry your eyes.
  Tears show their love but want their remedies.
  Cousin, I am too young to be your father,
  Though you are old enough to be my heir.
  What you will have I'll give, and willing too,   205
  For do we must what force will have us do.
  Set on towards London, cousin, is it so?
BULLINGBROOK Yea, my good lord.
RICHARD   Then I must not say no.

         Flourish. Exeunt

The queen and her ladies unhappily pace York's garden.

---

1 'God Almighty first planted a garden' Francis Bacon (in groups of four to five)

This scene is a strangely unique moment in the play, placed as it is between the momentous events at Flint Castle and the formal abdication of the king in the next scene.

Make a list of all the words (both good and bad) that occur to you when the word 'garden' is mentioned. Then take a part each and read the whole scene straight through. How are the two groups of people (queen + ladies and gardener + servants) contrasted? Talk about which of your 'garden associations' seem to be highlighted in this scene.

A late medieval garden.

---

rubs difficulties (in bowls a 'rub' was any impediment to the bowl)
bias the weight on the side of the bowl which makes it curve when rolled
measure 1 musical time, dance step 2 limit

wanting lacking
it boots not to complain there is no point in lamenting
I could sing . . . good if weeping were any help, I would be happy now

ACT 3 SCENE 4
The Duke of York's garden

Enter the QUEEN *with her attendants*

QUEEN What sport shall we devise here in this garden
    To drive away the heavy thought of care?
LADY Madam, we'll play at bowls.
QUEEN 'Twill make me think the world is full of rubs
    And that my fortune runs against the bias.   5
LADY Madam, we'll dance.
QUEEN My legs can keep no measure in delight
    When my poor heart no measure keeps in grief.
    Therefore no dancing, girl. Some other sport.
LADY Madam, we'll tell tales.   10
QUEEN Of sorrow or of joy?
LADY   Of either, madam.
QUEEN Of neither, girl.
    For if of joy, being altogether wanting
    It doth remember me the more of sorrow,
    Or if of grief, being altogether had   15
    It adds more sorrow to my want of joy.
    For what I have I need not to repeat
    And what I want it boots not to complain.
LADY Madam, I'll sing.
QUEEN   'Tis well that thou hast cause,
    But thou shouldst please me better wouldst thou weep.   20
LADY I could weep, Madam, would it do you good.
QUEEN And I could sing would weeping do me good,
    And never borrow any tear of thee.

The queen observes the gardeners at work. As she suspects, they talk of public affairs.

---

1 Be a gardener (in small groups)

It may not be possible to do much gardening on stage, particularly an Elizabethan stage, but the gardener's words are full of hard work!

Read the gardener's lines (lines 29–39) together twice. Then one person reads the lines slowly, pausing at the end of each sentence, while the rest mime the actions. This is best done standing up as if you were actually doing some gardening. See how many different activities you can mime.

Next, be a 'political gardener'. As one reads, the rest do a silent dramatisation of the gardener's words as if he were describing political events. This needs planning and rehearsal.

Take lines 29–66 and make two lists of words:

a words connected with gardening, growing, nature
b words connected with politics, government and England.

How many words appear in both lists? Should you include 'children' and 'sire'?

2 Echoes from the past

Do the words of the gardener and the servant remind you of any events in the play so far? Compare their picture of England with Gaunt's vision in 2.1. They are very similar yet very different.

3 Was Richard a good gardener?

Look at the picture of a late medieval garden on page 116. What, according to the gardener, should a well-run garden and a well-governed kingdom be like?

---

my ... unto I'll bet my wretchedness against ...
against a change when a change is about to happen
forerun heralded by
apricocks apricots

noisome harmful
in ... pale within the limits of a fence
firm estate strong government
knots patterned flower beds
suffered allowed, permitted

Enter a GARDENER *and two* SERVANTS.

But stay, here come the gardeners.
Let's step into the shadow of these trees.   25
My wretchedness unto a row of pins
They'll talk of state, for everyone doth so
Against a change. Woe is forerun with woe.
GARDENER Go bind thou up young dangling apricocks,
Which like unruly children make their sire   30
Stoop with oppression of their prodigal weight.
Give some supportance to the bending twigs.
Go thou, and like an executioner
Cut off the heads of too-fast-growing sprays
That look too lofty in our commonwealth.   35
All must be even in our government.
You thus employed, I will go root away
The noisome weeds which without profit suck
The soil's fertility from wholesome flowers.
SERVANT Why should we, in the compass of a pale,   40
Keep law and form and due proportion,
Showing as in a model our firm estate,
When our sea-wallèd garden, the whole land,
Is full of weeds, her fairest flowers choked up,
Her fruit trees all unpruned, her hedges ruined,   45
Her knots disordered and her wholesome herbs
Swarming with caterpillars?
GARDENER   Hold thy peace.
He that hath suffered this disordered spring
Hath now himself met with the fall of leaf.
The weeds which his broad spreading leaves did shelter,   50
That seemed in eating him to hold him up,
Are plucked up root and all by Bullingbrook.
I mean the Earl of Wiltshire, Bushy, Green.

*As the gardener blames Richard for failing to care for his kingdom,
the queen angrily confronts the three men.*

---

1 'Overproud in sap and blood' (in pairs)

Read lines 55–6, taking a sentence each. The gardener talks of
pruning and ringing. Ringing is the practice of cutting the bark of a
tree to encourage fruit growth by restricting the flow of sap.

What are the criticisms that the gardener makes of Richard's
political conduct? Are they justified?

2 The Garden of Eden

Adam and Eve were the first man and woman. Adam is sometimes
described as the first gardener. Read the queen's words (lines 72–80).
In what way is the queen's vision of the garden (or country) set against
the gardener's? Look again at lines 1–39 and see how the different
behaviour of these two groups of people reflects their different
attitudes to life.

3 The scales of fortune

The gardener, in his own way, expresses the essential pattern of the
whole play. Read lines 83–9 out loud with the script on the table in
front of you and your hands held out on either side as if weighing two
objects. As you read, sense the weight in each hand and watch King
Richard fall. In what sense might this image be not altogether
encouraging for Bullingbrook?

Remember this image when you come to Act 4.

---

confound destroy
crown of the tree and of the king
depressed brought low
'tis doubt it is feared
divine foretell

pressed refers to the torture of
putting weights on a man's chest if
he remained silent and refused to
give evidence
odds advantage
post hasten

SERVANT What, are they dead?
GARDENER   They are, and Bullingbrook
     Hath seized the wasteful king. Oh what pity is it   55
     That he had not so trimmed and dressed his land
     As we this garden! We at time of year
     Do wound the bark, the skin of our fruit trees,
     Lest being overproud in sap and blood
     With too much riches it confound itself.   60
     Had he done so to great and growing men
     They might have lived to bear and he to taste
     Their fruits of duty. Superfluous branches
     We lop away, that bearing boughs may live.
     Had he done so, himself had borne the crown   65
     Which waste of idle hours hath quite thrown down.
SERVANT What, think you then the king shall be deposed?
GARDENER Depressed he is already, and deposed
     'Tis doubt he will be. Letters came last night
     To a dear friend of the good Duke of York's   70
     That tell black tidings.
QUEEN Oh, I am pressed to death through want of speaking!
     Thou, old Adam's likeness set to dress this garden,
     How dares thy harsh rude tongue sound this unpleasing news?
     What Eve, what serpent hath suggested thee   75
     To make a second fall of cursèd man?
     Why dost thou say King Richard is deposed?
     Darest thou, thou little better thing than earth,
     Divine his downfall? Say where, when and how
     Camest thou by this ill tidings? Speak, thou wretch!   80
GARDENER Pardon me, madam. Little joy have I
     To breathe this news, yet what I say is true.
     King Richard he is in the mighty hold
     Of Bullingbrook. Their fortunes both are weighed.
     In your lord's scale is nothing but himself   85
     And some few vanities that make him light,
     But in the balance of great Bullingbrook
     Besides himself are all the English peers,
     And with that odds he weighs King Richard down.
     Post you to London and you'll find it so.   90
     I speak no more than everyone doth know.

The queen prepares to go to London to meet Richard and curses the gardener for bringing such bad news. The gardener resolves to plant a herb to commemorate this sad moment.

---

1 A gardener and a weeping queen (in groups of four)

We shall shortly see the formal deposition of Richard which will open the 'purple testament of bleeding war', not to be closed for eighty-five years.

Read the scene from line 67 to the end (there are two speaking parts plus servant and ladies). Work out (or block) the moves for these lines and walk them through. Include all the gestures and movements that the 'internal stage directions' reveal. It may help to 'point' clearly on saying words like 'thou', 'I', 'mischance', 'plants' (see page 8). Then rehearse a presentation to the rest of the class which tries to make clear the queen's reactions to the gardener and gardener's reactions to the queen.

What hope for the future does this simple, plain man offer us?

2 Write your own ending

Write your own version of the last six lines of this scene, but begin with 'Poor queen . . .'. Compose it either in blank verse with a concluding couplet, or entirely in couplets. You will probably have acquired a sense of the blank verse structure from your readings. If not, read pages 202–03.

---

embassage message
so that . . . no worse if it meant that your situation would be improved

rue garden herb, also called 'herb of grace' (usually associated with repentance but here the gardener links it with 'ruth' meaning 'pity')

QUEEN Nimble mischance, that art so light of foot,
     Doth not thy embassage belong to me,
     And am I last that knows it? Oh, thou thinkest
     To serve me last that I may longest keep   95
     Thy sorrow in my breast. Come ladies, go
     To meet at London London's king in woe.
     What, was I born to this, that my sad look
     Should grace the triumph of great Bullingbrook?
     Gardener, for telling me these news of woe   100
     Pray God the plants thou graft'st may never grow.
                         Exit [*with attendants*]
GARDENER Poor queen, so that thy state might be no worse
     I would my skill were subject to thy curse.
     Here did she fall a tear. Here in this place
     I'll set a bank of rue, sour herb of grace.   105
     Rue even for ruth here shortly shall be seen
     In the remembrance of a weeping queen.
                             Exeunt

Looking back at Act 3

What is to come in Act 4 is, in a sense, a formality, because politically Richard is finished. His belief in the sacred power of kingship was not enough. When the confrontation came he crumbled.

1 One-minute version

Devise, rehearse and present a one-minute potted version of the whole of Act 3, using your own dialogue or selected lines from the play.

2 Historic meeting

Devise and tape a radio broadcast by the BBC's political correspondent of the historic meeting of Richard and Bullingbrook at Flint Castle. Include interviews with some of the leading figures, but also interview some of the servants or soldiers. The common people have very little chance to put their points of view in this play.

3 Press statement

After a summit meeting, the two leaders generally meet the press, have their photographs taken and issue a press statement. Two of you take the roles of Richard and Bullingbrook while the others prepare to be members of the press or television (e.g. tabloid reporter, 'heavy' reporter, reporter from a foreign newspaper, BBC and ITV reporters). Question the two leaders and get as much out of them as you can.

4 Bullingbrook's diary

Richard describes Bullingbrook in the next act as the 'silent king', which is ironic in view of all his speeches in Acts 1 and 2. However, Richard is in a sense right, for Bullingbrook reveals no more than he has to of his real intentions. Write Bullingbrook's diary entry after the Flint Castle episode where he 'reveals all'.

5 Respect and status

Even the pronouns in the play can give important signals. Shakespeare often has social inferiors use the respectful 'you, yours' pronouns to superiors, while the 'thee, thou' pronouns are used to address social inferiors, children or friends. Look at how these pronouns are used in the garden scene (3.4). Why should the gardener use 'thy' in line 102?

6 Looking forward to Act 4

Bullingbrook hopes that a public transfer of power will ease men's minds. The handing over of the crown must appear both legitimate and voluntary, for there was no law by which men could legally depose their king.

Richard, however, is not yet finished. If Bullingbrook is going to make him play a game, then he will play it with a vengeance. The spirit of resistance, so lacking at Flint Castle, ironically returns now that it is too late.

All the great lords and bishops of England are present. Will they support Bullingbrook's accession to the throne? Look at the list of characters who enter for Scene 1 and decide how each one might feel as he watches the last moments of King Richard's reign.

7 Momentous changes

The single scene which makes up Act 4 includes a number of historical events which in fact extended over several months:

29 September 1399: Richard abdicates
30 September 1399: Bullingbrook takes the throne as Henry IV
16 October   1399: Bagot accuses Aumerle
22 October   1399: Carlisle speaks out in defence of Richard
27 October   1399: Henry decides to send for Mowbray
In December 1399: Abbot of Westminster begins his conspiracy.

Act 4 is short enough to be read through in one go, so do a preliminary read-through (sit in a circle if there is a group of you). Then try to divide up the scene into the different historical events listed above. Shakespeare has also changed their chronological order. What dramatic possibilities do you think this gives him?

A parliamentary meeting of the nobles, presided over by Bullingbrook, investigates the circumstances of Gloucester's death. Bagot accuses Aumerle of the murder.

1 The empty throne (in groups of six)

The king's Chair of State would be centre stage. Historical records say that it remained empty and was covered over with a cloth of gold. As the stage direction implies ('enter as to the Parliament'), this was not a legitimate assembly. Only the king could preside over a session of Parliament.

Three of the group take the roles of Bullingbrook, Bagot and Aumerle. The others act as the assembled nobles. Work out moves for lines 1–29 which highlight the visual and symbolic importance of the throne. In what ways does the opening of this scene echo 1.1 and 1.3?

2 A stormy start (in groups of eight)

Aumerle, Richard's cousin and close supporter of the king, has to face some angry lords. Choose a part each and find yourselves a 'glove'. Sit in a fairly large circle and read lines 1–106. Work through the whole series of challenges, throwing down your gloves and taking them up. Bullingbrook should stand in the centre and the other characters can stand (or enter the circle) when it is their turn to speak. Make this a stormy start and ask Aumerle how he feels when you get to line 106.

3 Who is telling the truth?

A familiar problem! Read Bagot's accusation against Aumerle (lines 8–19). Do you see any contradiction in what he says?

---

who wrought it with the king who persuaded the king (to murder Gloucester)
timeless end untimely
base man low-born (a knight was not bound to fight with a social inferior – see also 1.1.69–72)

chastisement punishment
attainder accusation
gage glove, gauntlet
manual . . . death Aumerle's gesture (throwing down the gauntlet) is the proof ('seal') that Bagot will die

ACT 4 SCENE 1
Westminster Hall

Enter as to the Parliament BULLINGBROOK, AUMERLE,
NORTHUMBERLAND, PERCY, FITZWATER, SURREY, the Bishop of
CARLISLE, the Abbot of WESTMINSTER, HERALD, Officers, and BAGOT

BULLINGBROOK Call forth Bagot.
        Now, Bagot, freely speak thy mind
        What thou dost know of noble Gloucester's death,
        Who wrought it with the king, and who performed
        The bloody office of his timeless end.   5
BAGOT Then set before my face the Lord Aumerle.
BULLINGBROOK Cousin, stand forth, and look upon that man.
BAGOT My Lord Aumerle, I know your daring tongue
        Scorns to unsay what once it hath delivered.
        In that dead time when Gloucester's death was plotted   10
        I heard you say 'Is not my arm of length,
        That reacheth from the restful English court
        As far as Calais, to mine uncle's head?'
        Amongst much other talk that very time
        I heard you say that you had rather refuse   15
        The offer of an hundred thousand crowns
        Than Bullingbrook's return to England,
        Adding withal how blessed this land would be
        In this your cousin's death.
AUMERLE   Princes and noble lords,
        What answer shall I make to this base man?   20
        Shall I so much dishonour my fair stars
        On equal terms to give him chastisement?
        Either I must, or have mine honour soiled
        With the attainder of his slanderous lips.
        There is my gage, the manual seal of death   25
        That marks thee out for hell. I say thou liest,
        And will maintain what thou hast said is false
        In thy heart blood, though being all too base
        To stain the temper of my knightly sword.

In defence, Aumerle challenges Bagot to Trial by Combat. Bullingbrook forbids Bagot to accept, whereupon several other nobles challenge Aumerle.

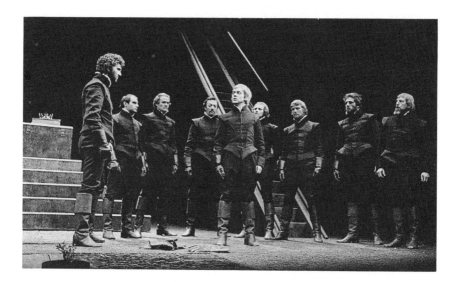

1 The challenges: comedy or menace?
(in groups of five or more)

Notice how Bullingbrook's supporters are all dressed in black in this production. Take up similar positions and create a menacing version of lines 25–90. Then present the same lines in a comic manner. Aumerle's stage business with the gages is interesting to work on here (especially line 83).

Historical records say that twenty-one challenges were made. Earlier in Richard's reign, 305 gages were tossed at the feet of one unfortunate knight. An observer wrote that the descending gloves 'looked like a fall of snow'.

---

excepting one/that fair sun to whom do these two rather uneasily flattering references refer?
stand on sympathy insists on equal rank (Fitzwater is also a lord)
vauntingly boastfully

appeal/honour's pawn the same ritual phrases as in 1.1 and 1.3
task burden (i.e. throw down another gage)
sun to sun sunrise to sunset was the formal time limit for a combat

BULLINGBROOK Bagot, forbear. Thou shalt not take it up.   30
AUMERLE Excepting one, I would he were the best
      In all this presence that hath moved me so.
FITZWATER If that thy valour stand on sympathy,
      There is my gage, Aumerle, in gage to thine.
      By that fair sun which shows me where thou standest   35
      I heard thee say, and vauntingly thou spak'st it,
      That thou wert cause of noble Gloucester's death.
      If thou deniest it twenty times, thou liest,
      And I will turn thy falsehood to thy heart
      Where it was forgèd, with my rapier's point.   40
AUMERLE Thou dar'st not, coward, live to see that day.
FITZWATER Now by my soul I would it were this hour.
AUMERLE Fitzwater, thou art damned to hell for this.
PERCY Aumerle, thou liest. His honour is as true
      In this appeal as thou art all unjust,   45
      And that thou art so, there I throw my gage,
      To prove it on thee to the extremest point
      Of mortal breathing. Seize it if thou darest.
AUMERLE And if I do not may my hands rot off
      And never brandish more revengeful steel   50
      Over the glittering helmet of my foe!
ANOTHER LORD I task the earth to the like, forsworn Aumerle,
      And spur thee on with full as many lies
      As may be hollowed in thy treacherous ear
      From sun to sun. There is my honour's pawn.   55
      Engage it to the trial if thou darest.
AUMERLE Who sets me else? By heaven, I'll throw at all!
      I have a thousand spirits in one breast
      To answer twenty thousand such as you.
SURREY My Lord Fitzwater, I do remember well   60
      The very time Aumerle and you did talk.
FITZWATER 'Tis very true, you were in presence then
      And you can witness with me this is true.

The arguments among the nobles threaten to get out of hand. Bullingbrook
orders them all to stop quarrelling until Mowbray is recalled from
banishment, only to be told that he is dead.

1 Mowbray the crusader (in groups of four)

One person reads the account by the Bishop of Carlisle of Mowbray's
death (lines 91–100). The rest mime together the story of Mowbray's
life after he was banished. What is emphasised here – militant
Christianity or pious devotion?

References to pilgrimages and crusades occur earlier in the play.
Making Mowbray a crusader seems to be entirely Shakespeare's
invention. Does this change your view of him in any way?

2 A concern for truth and justice?

Remember how Gaunt and York criticised Richard's favourites and
close advisers? Bullingbrook has already beheaded two of them and
now the lords make a ferocious attack on Aumerle and Surrey.
Bullingbrook's party has won, so why should there be so much
vindictiveness? If it still puzzles you, read pages 194–5.

3 How well does Bullingbrook cope?

Compare the way Bullingbrook sorts out these quarrelling lords with
the way in which Richard deals with Mowbray and Bullingbrook in
the opening scene of the play.

---

fondly foolishly, needlessly
forward eager, willing
appeal accusation
repealed brought back from exile
try his honour prove his honour

(Mowbray now looks set to fight
Aumerle!)
rest under gage wait to be resolved
signories estates
toiled exhausted by

SURREY As false, by heaven, as heaven itself is true.
FITZWATER Surrey, thou liest.
SURREY   Dishonourable boy,   65
    That lie shall lie so heavy on my sword
    That it shall render vengeance and revenge
    Till thou the lie-giver and that lie do lie
    In earth as quiet as thy father's skull.
    In proof whereof there is my honour's pawn.   70
    Engage it to the trial if thou darest.
FITZWATER How fondly dost thou spur a forward horse!
    If I dare eat or drink or breathe or live
    I dare meet Surrey in a wilderness
    And spit upon him whilst I say he lies   75
    And lies and lies. There is my bond of faith
    To tie thee to my strong correction.
    As I intend to thrive in this new world
    Aumerle is guilty of my true appeal.
    Besides, I heard the banished Norfolk say   80
    That thou, Aumerle, didst send two of thy men
    To execute the noble duke at Calais.
AUMERLE Some honest Christian trust me with a gage.
    That Norfolk lies, here do I throw down this,
    If he may be repealed to try his honour.   85
BULLINGBROOK These differences shall all rest under gage
    Till Norfolk be repealed. Repealed he shall be
    And, though mine enemy, restored again
    To all his lands and signories. When he's returned,
    Against Aumerle we will enforce his trial.   90
CARLISLE That honourable day shall ne'er be seen.
    Many a time hath banished Norfolk fought
    For Jesu Christ in glorious Christian field,
    Streaming the ensign of the Christian cross
    Against black pagans, Turks and Saracens,   95
    And, toiled with works of war, retired himself
    To Italy, and there at Venice gave
    His body to that pleasant country's earth
    And his pure soul unto his captain, Christ,
    Under whose colours he had fought so long.   100

*York appears to tell Bullingbrook that Richard has agreed to abdicate and
adopts him as his heir. The Bishop of Carlisle strongly protests.*

---

1 The Bishop of Carlisle speaks out (in groups of three)

Read the Bishop of Carlisle's speech (lines 114–49), taking a
sentence each in turn. Do this a second time but now address your
words very forcefully to the other two. Emphasise strongly every
'superior' or 'inferior' word (e.g. 'noble', or 'subject'). Talk about the
effect the bishop's words have on you.

Then memorise lines 112–16 and explore ways for the bishop to
prevent Bullingbrook from ascending the throne.

2 The heart of the problem

Just as it was not possible to hold a legal Parliament without the
presence of the king, so Bullingbrook and his supporters cannot
legally depose the king when the king himself is the source of all
justice.

The problem of removing Edward II was solved when the king was
'persuaded' to abdicate in favour of his son, Edward III (Richard's
grandfather). Is there anything in these lines which suggests that they
are hoping to convince Parliament that Richard has done the same?

List the main objections that Carlisle makes in lines 114–35 to this
rather dubious procedure.

Lords appellants a new batch of
them! (see pages 1–2)
worst most unfit, lowest in rank (a
mere priest amongst nobles)
best beseeming me I am best
qualified
noblesse nobility

learn him forbearance teach him
to refrain
but they are by except when they
are present
apparent obvious
forfend forbid, prevent

BULLINGBROOK Why, bishop, is Norfolk dead?

CARLISLE As surely as I live, my lord.

BULLINGBROOK Sweet peace conduct his sweet soul to the bosom
　　　　Of good old Abraham. Lords appellants,
　　　　Your differences shall all rest under gage　　　　　　　105
　　　　Till we assign you to your days of trial.

Enter YORK.

YORK Great Duke of Lancaster, I come to thee
　　　　From plume-plucked Richard, who with willing soul
　　　　Adopts thee heir, and his high sceptre yields
　　　　To the possession of thy royal hand.　　　　　　　　110
　　　　Ascend his throne, descending now from him,
　　　　And long live Henry, of that name the fourth!

BULLINGBROOK In God's name I'll ascend the regal throne.

CARLISLE Marry, God forbid!
　　　　Worst in this royal presence may I speak,　　　　　　115
　　　　Yet best beseeming me to speak the truth.
　　　　Would God that any in this noble presence
　　　　Were enough noble to be upright judge
　　　　Of noble Richard. Then true noblesse would
　　　　Learn him forbearance from so foul a wrong.　　　　　120
　　　　What subject can give sentence on his king,
　　　　And who sits here that is not Richard's subject?
　　　　Thieves are not judged but they are by to hear
　　　　Although apparent guilt be seen in them,
　　　　And shall the figure of God's majesty,　　　　　　　125
　　　　His captain, steward, deputy, elect,
　　　　Anointed, crownèd, planted many years,
　　　　Be judged by subject and inferior breath
　　　　And he himself not present? Oh, forfend it, God,
　　　　That in a Christian climate souls refined　　　　　　130
　　　　Should show so heinous, black, obscene a deed!
　　　　I speak to subjects and a subject speaks,
　　　　Stirred up by God thus boldly for his king.
　　　　My lord of Herford here, whom you call king,
　　　　Is a foul traitor to proud Herford's king,　　　　　　135

The Bishop of Carlisle warns that deposing the king will lead to dreadful civil war. Northumberland immediately arrests the bishop on charges of high treason. Richard is summoned to appear.

1 Prophetic words (in groups of four)

John of Gaunt (2.1.31–68) presented his vision of an England suffering under Richard's irresponsible rule. The Bishop of Carlisle now prophesies that England will also suffer if Richard's crown is usurped.

Try to create the bishop's vision of England's future. Take it in turns to read lines 136–49. The others echo words that strike them as prophesying disorder and chaos.

2 Moment of decision (in groups of eight)

Are the assembled nobles in any way swayed by Carlisle? At least three of those present are unhappy with events. Rehearse lines 136–61 in two ways:

a the assembled nobles support Carlisle as he speaks and are hostile to Northumberland, York and Bullingbrook

b everyone is silent and hostile to the bishop as he speaks.

Can you present the lines in any other ways?

3 Richard's last chance

Write down (perhaps as a poem) what you think Richard might be thinking as he is escorted into the Hall of Westminster (which ironically he himself had built).

---

kin . . . confound families and fellow countrymen will destroy each other

Golgotha Calvary (where Christ was crucified)

if you raise . . . this house if you divide the country

the commons' suit the request of the House of Commons (i.e. to publish the terms of Richard's abdication)

sureties . . . answer men who will guarantee that you will appear for trial

beholding indebted

Judas the apostle who betrayed Christ

And if you crown him let me prophesy:
The blood of English shall manure the ground
And future ages groan for this foul act.
Peace shall go sleep with Turks and infidels,
And in this seat of peace tumultuous wars   140
Shall kin with kin and kind with kind confound.
Disorder, horror, fear and mutiny
Shall here inhabit, and this land be called
The field of Golgotha and dead men's skulls.
Oh, if you raise this house against this house   145
It will the woefullest division prove
That ever fell upon this cursèd earth.
Prevent it, resist it, let it not be so,
Lest child, child's children, cry against you woe.
NORTHUMBERLAND Well have you argued, sir, and for your pains   150
Of capital treason we arrest you here.
My Lord of Westminster, be it your charge
To keep him safely till his day of trial.
May it please you, lords, to grant the commons' suit?
BULLINGBROOK Fetch hither Richard, that in common view   155
He may surrender. So we shall proceed
Without suspicion.
YORK   I will be his conduct.   *Exit*
BULLINGBROOK Lords, you that here are under our arrest,
Procure your sureties for your days of answer.
Little are we beholding to your love   160
And little looked for at your helping hands.

Enter RICHARD *and York.*

RICHARD Alack, why am I sent for to a king
Before I have shook off the regal thoughts
Wherewith I reigned? I hardly yet have learned
To insinuate, flatter, bow and bend my knee.   165
Give sorrow leave awhile to tutor me
To this submission. Yet I well remember
The favours of these men. Were they not mine?
Did they not sometime cry 'All hail' to me?
So Judas did to Christ, but he in twelve   170
Found truth in all but one, I in twelve thousand none.

Richard prepares to hand over his crown to Bullingbrook.

---

1 'Here cousin, seize the crown' (in pairs)

The all-important moment. How difficult does Richard make it? Improvise a crown (for example, a wire coathanger bent into the shape of a circle). Take lines 181–201 and explore ways for Richard to behave and Bullingbrook to react. Work out movements for lines 183–8. Do they remind you of any image in the garden scene (3.4)? Decide when Richard might relinquish his hold on the crown.

2 Which is which?

In this picture from the 1973 Royal Shakespeare Company production, who is Richard and who is Bullingbrook? The answer on pages 188–9 may surprise you!

---

clerk altar-server (who makes the responses, the 'amens', to the priest's prayers)
tirèd majesty dressed or clothed (is there another possible meaning?)

owes possesses
'tend attend
aye – no. No – aye Speak lines 200–01 rather than look at them and you will hear some of the different meanings

God save the king! Will no man say Amen?
Am I both priest and clerk? Well then, Amen.
God save the king, although I be not he,
And yet Amen if heaven do think him me.   175
To do what service am I sent for hither?
YORK To do that office of thine own good will
Which tirèd majesty did make thee offer,
The resignation of thy state and crown
To Henry Bullingbrook.   180
RICHARD Give me the crown. Here, cousin, seize the crown,
On this side my hand and on that side thine.
Now is this golden crown like a deep well
That owes two buckets, filling one another,
The emptier ever dancing in the air,   185
The other down, unseen and full of water.
That bucket, down and full of tears, am I,
Drinking my griefs whilst you mount up on high.
BULLINGBROOK I thought you had been willing to resign.
RICHARD My crown I am, but still my griefs are mine.   190
You may my glories and my state depose,
But not my griefs. Still am I king of those.
BULLINGBROOK Part of your cares you give me with your crown.
RICHARD Your cares set up do not pluck my cares down.
My care is loss of care, by old care done.   195
Your care is gain of care, by new care won.
The cares I give I have, though given away.
They 'tend the crown, yet still with me they stay.
BULLINGBROOK Are you contented to resign the crown?
RICHARD Aye – no. No – aye, for I must nothing be,   200
Therefore no 'no', for I resign to thee.

Richard ceremonially divests himself of all his royal powers.
Northumberland requests that he also reads a statement confessing to his
crimes. Richard refuses.

1 Richard's final ceremony (in groups of three)

Take the parts of Richard, Bullingbrook and the attendant who carries the crown and sceptre. Rehearse lines 202–21. Use a 'crown' if you have one. The attendant holds Richard's script in front of him so that he can read his lines and keep both hands free. Richard gives a significant movement or gesture to every line (it may at times be simply 'pointing'). Talk together about the mood or feeling that seems to be present at this moment both in the picture and in your particular version.

---

undo 1 undress **2** destroy.
  Can you see both meanings here?
balm anointing oil
make me . . . grieved (God) make
  me
  1 grieved by having nothing
  2 grieved by nothing

ravel out unravel or unweave.
  Try to picture the image Richard is
  using in lines 227–8
gentle 1 noble
  2 soft-mannered. What do you
  think of either meaning as applied
  to Northumberland?

Now, mark me how I will undo myself.
I give this heavy weight from off my head
And this unwieldy sceptre from my hand,
The pride of kingly sway from out my heart.   205
With mine own tears I wash away my balm;
With mine own hands I give away my crown;
With mine own tongue deny my sacred state;
With mine own breath release all duteous oaths.
All pomp and majesty I do forswear;   210
My manors, rents, revenues I forgo;
My acts, decrees, and statutes I deny.
God pardon all oaths that are broke to me;
God keep all vows unbroke are made to thee.
Make me that nothing have with nothing grieved,   215
And thou with all pleased that hast all achieved.
Long mayst thou live in Richard's seat to sit,
And soon lie Richard in an earthy pit.
God save King Henry, unkinged Richard says,
And send him many years of sunshine days.   220
What more remains?
NORTHUMBERLAND   No more, but that you read
These accusations and these grievous crimes
Committed by your person and your followers
Against the state and profit of this land,
That by confessing them the souls of men   225
May deem that you are worthily deposed.
RICHARD Must I do so? And must I ravel out
My weaved-up follies? Gentle Northumberland,
If thy offences were upon record
Would it not shame thee, in so fair a troop,   230
To read a lecture of them? If thou wouldst,
There shouldst thou find one heinous Article
Containing the deposing of a king
And cracking the strong warrant of an oath,
Marked with a blot, damned in the book of heaven.   235

Northumberland again asks Richard to read the document listing all his crimes. Richard refuses and asks the new king to send for a mirror.

1 'I have no name, no title' (in groups of four, six or eight)

Richard has just given away his crown and is beginning to realise the significance of what he has done.

First work in pairs, one as Richard one as Northumberland. Read lines 219–74. As he reads, Richard must say to whom he is speaking: the assembled company, particular nobles, or himself.

Next, join with the rest of the group and stand in a circle. Each of you choose a line spoken by Richard which seems particularly powerful or moving and speak it to the others. Then rehearse lines 219–74. Richard must 'point' or target all his words. Talk together about your feelings for Richard at this point and the reactions of those watching him. What reasons can you give for Richard's request for a mirror?

2 Sun, water, tears, names (individually or in small groups)

You will have sensed these images many times in the play. The echoes are heard again here.

Make a list of all words in lines 181–266 to do with sun, water, tears, and names. Why do these images now seem so much in Richard's mind?

3 'The commons will not then be satisfied'

There are at least six earlier references in this scene to the need for a show of legality. Can you find them?

---

bait torment (as in bull- or bear-baiting)

you Pilates Pontius Pilate judged Jesus. Richard compares himself to Christ (for the second time in this scene)

sort pack, or gang (contemptuous term)

pompous magnificent, splendid

state stateliness

at the font (i.e. at his christening)

and if if

sterling valid currency

ere before

Nay, all of you that stand and look upon me
Whilst that my wretchedness doth bait my self,
Though some of you with Pilate wash your hands,
Showing an outward pity, yet you Pilates
Have here delivered me to my sour cross   240
And water cannot wash away your sin.

NORTHUMBERLAND My lord, dispatch. Read o'er these Articles.

RICHARD Mine eyes are full of tears; I cannot see.
And yet salt water blinds them not so much
But they can see a sort of traitors here.   245
Nay, if I turn mine eyes upon my self
I find myself a traitor with the rest,
For I have given here my soul's consent
T'undeck the pompous body of a king,
Made glory base, a sovereignty a slave,   250
Proud majesty a subject, state a peasant.

NORTHUMBERLAND My lord –

RICHARD No lord of thine, thou haught insulting man,
Nor no man's lord. I have no name, no title,
No, not that name was given me at the font,   255
But 'tis usurped. Alack the heavy day
That I have worn so many winters out
And know not now what name to call myself.
Oh that I were a mockery king of snow
Standing before the sun of Bullingbrook,   260
To melt myself away in water drops.
Good king, great king, and yet not greatly good,
And if my word be sterling yet in England
Let it command a mirror hither straight
That it may show me what a face I have   265
Since it is bankrupt of his majesty.

BULLINGBROOK Go some of you, and fetch a looking glass.
                          [*Exit an attendant*]

NORTHUMBERLAND Read o'er this paper while the glass doth come.

RICHARD Fiend, thou torments me ere I come to hell.

BULLINGBROOK Urge it no more, my Lord Northumberland.   270

NORTHUMBERLAND The commons will not then be satisfied.

RICHARD They shall be satisfied. I'll read enough
When I do see the very book indeed
Where all my sins are writ, and that's my self.

Richard takes the mirror and gazes at his own face. Then smashes the glass.
He asks Bullingbrook for one final favour.

1 **'When I want to look at a**
   fool I have only to look in
   the mirror.' Seneca
   (in groups of four)

Find a mirror and look at
yourself for a moment. Think
about what you expect to see and
what you actually see. Then read
the opposite page through, taking
a sentence each in turn. Talk
about what you think Richard
expects to see in the mirror and
what he actually sees.

2 **What comment is this**
   production making here?

wink close their eyes
faced covered over, condoned (a
  pun. Literally to cover or trim a
  garment with new cloth)

outfaced overcome
to the unseen grief compared with
  the unseen grief
boon favour

Enter one with a glass.

Give me that glass and therein will I read.   275
No deeper wrinkles yet? Hath sorrow struck
So many blows upon this face of mine
And made no deeper wounds? Oh flattering glass,
Like to my followers in prosperity
Thou dost beguile me. Was this face the face   280
That every day under his household roof
Did keep ten thousand men? Was this the face
That like the sun did make beholders wink?
Is this the face which faced so many follies,
That was at last outfaced by Bullingbrook?   285
A brittle glory shineth in this face.
As brittle as the glory is the face,
                    [*Smashes the glass.*]
For there it is, cracked in an hundred shivers.
Mark, silent king, the moral of this sport,
How soon my sorrow hath destroyed my face.   290
BULLINGBROOK The shadow of your sorrow hath destroyed
    The shadow of your face.
RICHARD   Say that again.
    The shadow of my sorrow. Ha, let's see.
    'Tis very true, my grief lies all within
    And these external manners of laments   295
    Are merely shadows to the unseen grief
    That swells with silence in the tortured soul.
    There lies the substance; and I thank thee, king,
    For thy great bounty, that not only givest
    Me cause to wail but teachest me the way   300
    How to lament the cause. I'll beg one boon
    And then be gone and trouble you no more.
    Shall I obtain it?
BULLINGBROOK   Name it, fair cousin.
RICHARD Fair cousin? I am greater than a king,
    For when I was a king my flatterers   305
    Were then but subjects. Being now a subject
    I have a king here to my flatterer.
    Being so great I have no need to beg.

Bullingbrook and the assembled nobles depart with Richard. The Bishop of Westminster, the Duke of Aumerle and the Bishop of Carlisle are left to plot against the new king.

1 Sorrows and shadows (in pairs)

Memorise lines 289–92, one person Richard, one as Bullingbrook. Sit facing each other and say your lines to each other several times. Explore different ways of expressing the words. What is Richard trying to tell Bullingbrook and what is Bullingbrook trying to tell Richard?

This is the last time that these two great rivals speak to each other. Have a pen and paper ready beside you. Speak lines 309–14 several times, looking into your partner's eyes. Try each time to express all the different thoughts you have at this moment. Quickly write your thoughts down – don't worry how or what you write, just let the words flow out in a fast and almost unconscious fashion. Read to each other what you have written. Use these thoughts as the basis for a poem.

2 'A plot shall show us all a merry day' (in groups of three)

Do not be too surprised to see men of the church so involved in politics. The church held large amounts of land. Like the nobility, it was expected to supply the king with armed soldiers when the country went to war. The House of Lords included many powerful church figures.

Read lines 320–33, taking a part each. Talk about how an audience might feel as the reign of Henry IV begins. Do you sense any echoes of an earlier scene?

---

convey usually meant 'to escort' but could also mean 'to transfer the legal title to a property' (i.e. conveyancing) or 'to steal'. Can you see how all three meanings apply here?

pageant spectacle
blot remember Gaunt's 'inky blots' in 2.1.64? Who else uses the word in this scene?
take . . . intents swear a religious oath or promise (sacrament) to conceal my plans

BULLINGBROOK Yet ask.

RICHARD And shall I have?   310

BULLINGBROOK You shall.

RICHARD Then give me leave to go.

BULLINGBROOK Whither?

RICHARD Whither you will, so I were from your sights.

BULLINGBROOK Go some of you, convey him to the Tower.   315

RICHARD Oh good – 'convey'. Conveyers are you all
 That rise thus nimbly by a true king's fall.

BULLINGBROOK On Wednesday next we solemnly set down
 Our coronation. Lords, prepare yourselves.

     Exeunt [Bullingbrook, Richard, Lords and guards,
     all except] Westminster, Carlisle and Aumerle

WESTMINSTER A woeful pageant have we here beheld.   320

CARLISLE The woe's to come. The children yet unborn
 Shall feel this day as sharp to them as thorn.

AUMERLE You holy clergymen, is there no plot
 To rid the realm of this pernicious blot?

WESTMINSTER My lord,   325
 Before I freely speak my mind herein
 You shall not only take the sacrament
 To bury mine intents but also to effect
 Whatever I shall happen to devise.
 I see your brows are full of discontent,   330
 Your hearts of sorrow and your eyes of tears.
 Come home with me to supper. I will lay
 A plot shall show us all a merry day.

            Exeunt

Looking back at Act 4

Richard has been made to relinquish the crown. The unthinkable has happened, and Richard has made it abundantly clear that what has taken place is truly wrong.

We've seen the vivid picture of two crownless kings with the 'hollow crown' between them. Each is a king and yet not a king. The strangest thing of all is that Richard loses everything while Bullingbrook gains everything, but it is Richard who grows in stature while Bullingbrook becomes ever more silent.

1 A dumb show

'A woeful pageant have we here beheld' says the Abbot of Westminster at the end of Act 4. Devise a dumb show presentation of the whole act lasting just a few minutes. Try to convey the feelings of the different watchers as well as those of the main characters. It may help to record the major moves in note form first and then work from your notes.

2 An assessment of King Richard

As he is led away, Richard condemns the lords for bringing about 'a true king's fall'. Do you believe he is 'a true king'? Think about the impression he makes on you in Act 4 and compare it with his behaviour in Acts 1, 2 and 3. It may help to assess him using the following headings:

Richard the king
Richard the Christ-figure
Richard the actor
Richard the man
Richard the poet.

3 York's story

In Act 5, York recounts to his wife the story of how Richard was brought to London as prisoner of Bullingbrook. Write an account of how he might have told his wife of King Richard's deposition. How would he attempt to justify his own part in the proceedings?

4 Animals

One production dressed Northumberland to look like 'a great black raven in a feather cloak with claws on his buskined feet'. Take three or four characters and think about what animals or birds they might resemble. Make a drawing of one and write a short note about why you see him or her as your particular animal or bird. Are there any clues in the script to help you?

5 Write a ballad

Travelling minstrels no doubt composed ballads telling the story of Richard and Bullingbrook. Write your version.

6 A sense of place

You will need a map of England for this. More often than he usually does in his plays, Shakespeare has suggested in the dialogue the locality of each scene, for example, 2.3.1–3. It was these clues that later editors used when they added the scene headings. Start with Act 1 Scene 1 and trace the changing localities as the story unfolds. In particular, follow Bullingbrook's movements after he lands at Ravenspurgh.

7 Looking forward to Act 5

Richard likened the crown to a well with two buckets. The crown is certainly a well of instruction for both men. In Act 5 we see what Richard learns and what he becomes as he descends to the bottom of the well. We see also the new King Henry IV begin to realise the price he will have to pay for his triumph.

Loyalty, which has been a constant preoccupation for some characters, becomes an even more pressing dilemma. Since we now have two kings, which one is the real king? Which king is truly royal? Northumberland, York, York's wife, Aumerle, and Richard's former groom are all shown adjusting to the new regime and new loyalties. Not even Richard's horse can escape judgement.

The queen waits to speak with her husband as he is escorted to the Tower.

---

1 What can the queen do? (in groups of four to six)

The queen is doing what she can to help her husband. Each person chooses a sentence or phrase from lines 26–34 and speaks it in turn to the others, trying to rouse them to action.

Next, work out the moves for lines 1–17 so that the queen takes the initiative wherever possible (remember the guard). Look for the 'internal stage directions'. For example, decide what the queen does which prompts Richard to say 'Join not with grief, fair woman, do not so' (line 16).

Rehearse a presentation of lines 1–34 to show to the rest of the class.

2 A new Richard?

Almost at the moment of losing real power, Richard seems to gain another kind of majesty. Bullingbrook and York compared Richard to the sun and to an eagle (3.3.62–70). Find the two images in lines 1–34 that the queen uses to describe her husband (one of which echoes the garden scene).

What images in lines 16–25 suggest that in his misfortune Richard has acquired a new wisdom?

3 Parting (in groups of three)

This is the last we see of Richard's queen. Take a part each and read the whole scene through. Talk about the part she has played in these historic events. In what ways is her role in the play like that of the Duchess of Gloucester (1.2)?

Julius . . . tower the Tower of London (traditionally believed to have been built by Julius Caesar)
the model . . . stand you are like the ruins ('model') or the mere outline ('map') of a great city

old Troy legend had it that London was founded by a band of Trojans after the Trojan war
keep a league maintain an alliance
profane wicked

London   A street leading to the Tower

Enter the QUEEN *with her attendants*

QUEEN This way the king will come. This is the way
   To Julius Caesar's ill-erected tower,
   To whose flint bosom my condemnèd lord
   Is doomed a prisoner by proud Bullingbrook.
   Here let us rest, if this rebellious earth   5
   Have any resting for her true king's queen.

     Enter RICHARD *and guard.*

   But soft, but see, or rather do not see
   My fair rose wither. Yet look up, behold,
   That you in pity may dissolve to dew
   And wash him fresh again with true love tears.   10
   Ah thou, the model where old Troy did stand,
   Thou map of honour, thou King Richard's tomb,
   And not King Richard! Thou most beauteous inn,
   Why should hard-favoured grief be lodged in thee
   When triumph is become an alehouse guest?   15
RICHARD Join not with grief, fair woman, do not so,
   To make my end too sudden. Learn, good soul,
   To think our former state a happy dream,
   From which awaked, the truth of what we are
   Shows us but this. I am sworn brother, sweet,   20
   To grim Necessity, and he and I
   Will keep a league till death. Hie thee to France
   And cloister thee in some religious house.
   Our holy lives must win a new world's crown
   Which our profane hours here have thrown down.   25
QUEEN What, is my Richard both in shape and mind
   Transformed and weakenèd? Hath Bullingbrook
   Deposed thine intellect? Hath he been in thy heart?
   The lion dying thrusteth forth his paw
   And wounds the earth if nothing else with rage   30
   To be o'erpowered, and wilt thou, pupil-like,
   Take the correction mildly, kiss the rod,

*Northumberland informs Richard that Bullingbrook's plans have changed.
Richard is to be taken to Pomfret Castle.*

1 Still the old Richard? (in pairs)

Read Richard's words to his queen (lines 35–50), taking a sentence
each. Explore different ways of saying these lines (defiantly, laugh-
ingly, sadly, and so on). Is there an appropriate way to say them?

Compare the way he speaks here with his language in Acts 3 and 4.

2 Prophecy (in groups of four)

You will have witnessed Richard's outbursts before. Look at lines
51–70. Now he turns on Northumberland, the man most responsible
for helping Bullingbrook to the crown. Read lines 51–70, taking a
sentence each. What exactly does Richard prophesy?

which art a lion who is a lion
betid happened
ere before
'quite their griefs answer, or
match their tragic tales
for why! because
senseless unfeeling

brands burning logs
Pomfret Pontefract in Yorkshire
(centre of Bullingbrook's power)
order ta'en arrangements have
been made
worthy danger justifiable danger

And fawn on rage with base humility,
Which art a lion and the king of beasts?
RICHARD A king of beasts indeed. If aught but beasts   35
I had been still a happy king of men.
Good sometime queen, prepare thee hence for France.
Think I am dead, and that even here thou takest
As from my deathbed thy last living leave.
In winter's tedious nights sit by the fire   40
With good old folks, and let them tell thee tales
Of woeful ages long ago betid,
And ere thou bid good night, to 'quite their griefs
Tell thou the lamentable tale of me
And send the hearers weeping to their beds.   45
For why! the senseless brands will sympathise
The heavy accent of thy moving tongue,
And in compassion weep the fire out,
And some will mourn in ashes, some coal black,
For the deposing of a rightful king.   50

Enter NORTHUMBERLAND.

NORTHUMBERLAND My lord, the mind of Bullingbrook is changed.
You must to Pomfret, not unto the Tower.
And, madam, there is order ta'en for you.
With all swift speed you must away to France.
RICHARD Northumberland, thou ladder wherewithal   55
The mounting Bullingbrook ascends my throne,
The time shall not be many hours of age
More than it is ere foul sin gathering head
Shall break into corruption. Thou shalt think
Though he divide the realm and give thee half   60
It is too little, helping him to all.
He shall think that thou which knowest the way
To plant unrightful kings wilt know again,
Being ne'er so little urged, another way
To pluck him headlong from the usurpèd throne.   65
The love of wicked men converts to fear,
That fear to hate, and hate turns one or both
To worthy danger and deservèd death.
NORTHUMBERLAND My guilt be on my head, and there an end.
Take leave and part, for you must part forthwith.   70

Richard takes leave of his queen.

1 Separation

Having uncrowned himself in Act 4, Richard performs another inverted ceremony and 'unkisses' the marriage vow he made to his young queen.

The harshness of separation is expressed in lines 71–80. Make two columns of 'separates' and put as many words as you can into either column (for example 'marriage' and 'divorced').

2 Shared suffering, parted love (in groups of three)

The pain of parting and separation. The closeness of love and marriage. Show how these feelings are expressed through the verse (particularly the couplets) and through the actions of kissing and joining hands.

a Shared suffering

Take a part each and read lines 81–102. Talk together about how the words and couplets help you to hear and feel the closeness. What is the effect of hearing Northumberland take part in this exchange?

b Parted love

Imagine that Richard is bound or restrained in some way (one production had him held by a long chain around his neck). Have Northumberland acting as guard. Look in the language for the 'internal stage directions' and block the movements for this parting scene (lines 81–102). For example, how many times do they kiss or take hands? See what picture you create, then freeze one of the moments in your version and show it to the rest of the class as a tableau. Ask them to guess which line it refers to.

pines the clime afflicts the climate
Hollowmas Hallowmas, All Saints' Day (1 November)
little policy bad politics

than, near, be ne'er the near than nearby but never able to see each other
wanton unrestrained
fond tender and foolish

RICHARD Doubly divorced! Bad men, you violate
    A twofold marriage twixt my crown and me
    And then betwixt me and my married wife.
    Let me unkiss the oath twixt thee and me –
    And yet not so, for with a kiss 'twas made.   75
    Part us, Northumberland: I towards the north
    Where shivering cold and sickness pines the clime,
    My wife to France, from whence set forth in pomp
    She came adornèd hither like sweet May,
    Sent back like Hollowmas or short'st of day.   80
QUEEN And must we be divided? Must we part?
RICHARD Ay, hand from hand, my love, and heart from heart.
QUEEN Banish us both, and send the king with me.
NORTHUMBERLAND That were some love, but little policy.
QUEEN Then whither he goes thither let me go.   85
RICHARD So two together weeping make one woe.
    Weep thou for me in France, I for thee here;
    Better far off than, near, be ne'er the near.
    Go, count thy way with sighs, I mine with groans.
QUEEN So longest way shall have the longest moans.   90
RICHARD Twice for one step I'll groan, the way being short,
    And piece the way out with a heavy heart.
    Come, come, in wooing sorrow let's be brief
    Since, wedding it, there is such length in grief.
    One kiss shall stop our mouths, and dumbly part.   95
    Thus give I mine, and thus take I thy heart.
QUEEN Give me mine own again. 'Twere no good part
    To take on me to keep and kill thy heart.
    So, now I have mine own again be gone,
    That I may strive to kill it with a groan.   100
RICHARD We make woe wanton with this fond delay.
    Once more adieu, the rest let sorrow say.

                             Exeunt

The Duke of York sadly recounts to his wife the occasion of Bullingbrook and Richard's entrance to the city of London.

1 Bullingbrook enters London to cheers from citizens (in pairs)

Some nineteenth-century productions turned this scene into an elaborate stage spectacle. You will have to do it with the words alone!

Take it in turns to tell the duchess the story of Bullingbrook and Richard's entry into London (lines 1–40). Compare it with the description of Bullingbrook's journey into exile (1.4.24–36). Describe your feelings about Bullingbrook in his triumph and Richard in his failure.

A contemporary drawing of the event.

rude brutal
casements windows
visage face

painted imagery painted cloths depicting people with words coming out of their mouths were often hung on the walls during pageants and celebrations

ACT 5 SCENE 2
The Duke of York's house

Enter Duke of YORK and the DUCHESS

DUCHESS My lord, you told me you would tell the rest,
      When weeping made you break the story off,
      Of our two cousins coming into London.
YORK Where did I leave?
DUCHESS   At that sad stop, my lord,
      Where rude misgoverned hands from windows' tops   5
      Threw dust and rubbish on King Richard's head.
YORK Then, as I said, the duke, great Bullingbrook,
      Mounted upon a hot and fiery steed
      Which his aspiring rider seemed to know,
      With slow but stately pace kept on his course,   10
      Whilst all tongues cried 'God save thee, Bullingbrook!'
      You would have thought the very windows spake,
      So many greedy looks of young and old
      Through casements darted their desiring eyes
      Upon his visage, and that all the walls   15
      With painted imagery had said at once
      'Jesu preserve thee! Welcome, Bullingbrook!'
      Whilst he from one side to the other turning,
      Bare headed, lower than his proud steed's neck,
      Bespake them thus: 'I thank you, countrymen',   20
      And thus still doing, thus he passed along.

As York tells the duchess of the hostile reception that Richard received, he is interrupted by his son, Aumerle, now relegated to the rank of Earl of Rutland.

1 New loyalties, old loyalties (in groups of three)

Richard prophesied Northumberland's future treachery in the previous scene. Here, the whole question of loyalty becomes ever more troubling and complicated. Read the whole scene through together, taking one part each, and talk about the ways in which different characters view the question of loyalty. How is Henry, like Richard before him, attempting to encourage loyalty to the crown?

2 'After a well-graced actor leaves the stage'

York uses the theatrical image of actors entering and leaving the stage to describe the different receptions of Bullingbrook and Richard. Review the behaviour of the two men throughout the play so far. Which man has been the better actor?

3 'Who are the violets now?'

Aumerle has presumably just come from court. Read page 194 for an account of how and why Aumerle lost his title and see if it explains what the duchess means by her remark in lines 46–7.

bound our calm contents we willingly agree
for aye forever
truth loyalty
fealty faithfulness

had as lief would as willingly
do these . . . hold? will these tournaments and processions still take place?

DUCHESS Alack, poor Richard. Where rode he the whilst?
YORK As in a theatre the eyes of men
    After a well-graced actor leaves the stage
    Are idly bent on him that enters next,   25
    Thinking his prattle to be tedious,
    Even so or with much more contempt men's eyes
    Did scowl on Richard. No man cried 'God save him',
    No joyful tongue gave him his welcome home,
    But dust was thrown upon his sacred head,   30
    Which with such gentle sorrow he shook off,
    His face still combating with tears and smiles,
    The badges of his grief and patience,
    That had not God for some strong purpose steeled
    The hearts of men they must perforce have melted   35
    And barbarism itself have pitied him.
    But heaven hath a hand in these events,
    To whose high will we bound our calm contents.
    To Bullingbrook are we sworn subjects now,
    Whose state and honour I for aye allow.   40

Enter AUMERLE.

DUCHESS Here comes my son Aumerle.
YORK   Aumerle that was,
    But that is lost for being Richard's friend,
    And, madam, you must call him Rutland now.
    I am in Parliament pledge for his truth
    And lasting fealty to the new-made king.   45
DUCHESS Welcome, my son. Who are the violets now
    That strew the green lap of the new-come spring?
AUMERLE Madam, I know not, nor I greatly care not.
    God knows I had as lief be none as one.
YORK Well, bear you well in this new spring of time   50
    Lest you be cropped before you come to prime.
    What news from Oxford? Do these jousts and triumphs hold?
AUMERLE For aught I know, my lord, they do.
YORK You will be there, I know.
AUMERLE If God prevent it not I purpose so.   55

York discovers a document hidden inside Aumerle's shirt which shows that his son is involved in a plot to kill the new king at Oxford.

---

1 'Give me my boots, I say!' (in groups of four)

See how the stage springs to life in a way quite untypical of the play so far.

Take lines 41–116 (from the entrance of Aumerle to the end of the scene). There are three speaking parts plus the servant (who is silent but whose reactions could be very interesting!).

Take a part each and let the person playing Aumerle stick a roll of paper inside their shirt ready to be discovered. Look for the 'internal stage directions' and block the movements. For example, to whom does York speak line 74 or the duchess speak line 86?

You will notice that the servant enters with York's boots at line 84 and that York exits at line 109 presumably now wearing them. They would be long leather riding boots for travelling and very difficult to get on. Decide when York manages to get his boots from the servant. The duchess and Aumerle must see to it that he finds it very difficult to put them on.

When you have blocked this scene, put your scripts down and do it from memory, improvising the words but keeping as close to your original moves as you can. Play the scene for comedy and then play it seriously. Remember that Aumerle's life is at stake here.

Write director's notes for the cast on how they should play this scene.

---

without outside
band bond (the duchess assumes it is a bond for a loan of money). Remember Gaunt's 'oath and band' (1.1.2) and his 'rotten parchment bonds' (2.1.64)

gay apparel fine clothes
'gainst in readiness for
appeach inform against, or publicly accuse

YORK What seal is that that hangs without thy bosom?
      Yea, lookst thou pale? Let me see the writing.
AUMERLE My lord, 'tis nothing.
YORK   No matter then who see it.
      I will be satisfied. Let me see the writing.
AUMERLE I do beseech your grace to pardon me.   60
      It is a matter of small consequence,
      Which for some reasons I would not have seen.
YORK Which for some reasons, sir, I mean to see.
      I fear, I fear —
DUCHESS   What should you fear?
      'Tis nothing but some band that he is entered into   65
      For gay apparel 'gainst the triumph day.
YORK Bound to himself? What doth he with a bond
      That he is bound to? Wife, thou art a fool.
      Boy, let me see the writing.
AUMERLE I do beseech you pardon me. I may not show it.   70
YORK I will be satisfied. Let me see it, I say.
          He plucks it out of his bosom and reads it.
YORK Treason, foul treason! Villain! Traitor! Slave!
DUCHESS What's the matter, my lord?
YORK Ho, who's within there? Saddle my horse!
      God for His mercy, what treachery is here!   75
DUCHESS Why, what is't, my lord?
YORK Give me my boots, I say! Saddle my horse!
      Now by mine honour, by my life, my troth,
      I will appeach the villain.
DUCHESS   What is the matter?
YORK Peace, foolish woman!   80
DUCHESS I will not peace. What is the matter, Aumerle?
AUMERLE Good mother, be content. It is no more
      Than my poor life must answer.
DUCHESS   Thy life answer?
YORK Bring me my boots! I will unto the king.

York, Aumerle and the duchess all hasten to be first to reach the king.

---

1 Loyalty, disloyalty

Try to work out all the different combinations of loyalty and disloyalty shown by the three characters in this scene. For example, Aumerle is 'loyal' to Richard but 'disloyal' to Bullingbrook.

Loyalty is a question that has plagued York since Act 2 Scene 1. Talk about the different occasions when York has been faced with conflicts of loyalty. Then look at lines 44–5. Do they explain why his attitude here to his son's disloyalty is so different from his attitude to Bullingbrook's when he returned from banishment?

2 What will happen next? (individually or in small groups)

Predict what will happen when York, Aumerle and the duchess reach the king. Better still, improvise the scene.

3 What do the servants think? (in pairs)

The nobility in this play take themselves very seriously. What does the ordinary man think of them? Imagine you are the servant who witnessed this scene and tell your fellow servant all about it.

---

villain way of addressing a servant
teeming date time during which a woman can have children
interchangeably set down their hands each conspirator had a document signed by all the others

groaned in childbirth (the historical duchess was Aumerle's stepmother. Why the change?)
spur post ride quickly

His man enters with his boots.

DUCHESS Strike him, Aumerle! Poor boy, thou art amazed.   85
        Hence, villain! Never more come in my sight.
YORK Give me my boots, I say.
DUCHESS   Why York, what wilt thou do?
        Wilt thou not hide the trespass of thine own?
        Have we more sons, or are we like to have?
        Is not my teeming date drunk up with time,   90
        And wilt thou pluck my fair son from mine age
        And rob me of a happy mother's name?
        Is he not like thee? Is he not thine own?
YORK Thou fond mad woman,
        Wilt thou conceal this dark conspiracy?   95
        A dozen of them here have ta'en the sacrament
        And interchangeably set down their hands
        To kill the king at Oxford.
DUCHESS   He shall be none.
        We'll keep him here, then what is that to him?
YORK Away, fond woman! Were he twenty times my son   100
        I would appeach him.
DUCHESS   Hadst thou groaned for him
        As I have done thou wouldst be more pitiful.
        But now I know thy mind – thou dost suspect
        That I have been disloyal to thy bed
        And that he is a bastard, not thy son.   105
        Sweet York, sweet husband, be not of that mind.
        He is as like thee as a man may be,
        Not like to me or any of my kin,
        And yet I love him.
YORK   Make way, unruly woman!   *Exit*
DUCHESS After, Aumerle! Mount thee upon his horse,   110
        Spur post, and get before him to the king
        And beg thy pardon ere he do accuse thee.
        I'll not be long behind. Though I be old
        I doubt not but to ride as fast as York,
        And never will I rise up from the ground   115
        Till Bullingbrook have pardoned thee. Away, be gone.
                              Exeunt

*As King Henry asks Percy for news of his son who has been frequenting
the taverns and brothels of London, Aumerle enters, desperate to
speak with the king.*

1 'In this new world' (in pairs)

Just as it was not easy to know exactly where this play begins, so it is
not easy to know exactly where it ends. The first part of this scene in
fact looks forward to the story of Prince Hal (Bullingbrook's son)
dramatised in *Henry IV Part 1* and may indeed have been written for
this purpose. The historical alterations Shakespeare made suggest
that he had some plan in mind. For example, the historical Prince Hal
was only twelve at this time – rather young to be frequenting brothels!

Read lines 1–23, taking a part each. What do you think the world of
Henry IV will be like in *Henry IV Parts 1 and 2*?

2 Is Prince Hal another King Richard?

Just as this play looks forward in time, so the Henry IV plays
continually hark back to the reign of King Richard. Henry IV, at one
point, tells Prince Hal that he is behaving very much like King
Richard. Just how much alike are the two men judging by what you
learn of Prince Hal here?

3 Are Richard and Carlisle's prophecies coming true?

Read the prophecies that Richard and Carlisle make (3.3.91–100 and
4.1.136–49). What signs are there in this scene that Bullingbrook
himself is beginning to believe the prophecies might be coming true?

---

unthrifty extravagant and
  debauched
watch night-watchmen
passengers travellers
wanton unrestrained, reckless
  (compare with the 'unstaid youth'
  of Richard in 2.1.2)

takes . . . honour makes it a test of
  his kind of honour
stews brothels
wear it as a favour knights at
  tournaments wore a token (favour)
  given to them by a lady

ACT 5 SCENE 3
Windsor Castle

Enter BULLINGBROOK (*as king*), PERCY *and other lords*

BULLINGBROOK Can no man tell of my unthrifty son?
'Tis full three months since I did see him last.
If any plague hang over us 'tis he.
I would to God, my lords, he might be found.
Enquire at London 'mongst the taverns there,   5
For there they say he daily doth frequent
With unrestrainèd loose companions,
Even such, they say, as stand in narrow lanes
And beat our watch and rob our passengers,
Whilst he, young, wanton and effeminate boy,   10
Takes on the point of honour to support
So dissolute a crew.
PERCY My lord, some two days since I saw the prince
And told him of those triumphs held at Oxford.
BULLINGBROOK And what said the gallant?   15
PERCY His answer was he would unto the stews
And from the commonest creature pluck a glove
And wear it as a favour, and with that
He would unhorse the lustiest challenger.
BULLINGBROOK As dissolute as desperate! Yet through both   20
I see some sparks of better hope in him
Which elder years may happily bring forth.
But who comes here?

Enter AUMERLE *amazed.*

AUMERLE   Where is the king?
BULLINGBROOK   What means
Our cousin, that he stares and looks so wildly?
AUMERLE God save your grace. I do beseech your majesty   25
To have some conference with your grace alone.
BULLINGBROOK Withdraw yourselves, and leave us here alone.
                              [*Exeunt Percy and lords*]

Aumerle begins to beg for pardon, but before he can tell his story, York demands entry and shows King Henry the conspiracy document.

1 Father against son (in groups of four)

In another series of historical plays (the *Henry VI* cycle), Shakespeare includes a scene which presents the effects of civil war. It shows a son carrying his dead father, whom he has just slain, and then a father enters with his dead son.

Take a part each and read from the entrance of Aumerle (line 23) to the end of the scene. You will see a similar idea being developed here.

2 Staging Aumerle and York's meeting with the king (in groups of three)

The first few months of Henry's reign were quite insecure. According to the historical records, when Henry discovered the Abbot of Westminster's conspiracy, he fled with his family from Windsor to London, where the city fortunately stood by him.

Block the basic moves for lines 23–57. Look for the 'internal stage directions'. For example, can you work out where Aumerle probably rises from his knees? How do you know that York is out of breath?

What do you think of the behaviour of these three men?

ere before
how heinous e'er it be however
   hateful it may be
I'll make thee safe I'll render you
   harmless (how will he do it?)
secure over-confident

for love . . . treason out of my love
   for you call you a fool
my haste lack of breath caused by
   hurrying
confederate in agreement with
my hand my signature

What is the matter with our cousin now?

AUMERLE For ever may my knees grow to the earth, [*Kneels.*]
    My tongue cleave to the roof within my mouth,   30
    Unless a pardon ere I rise or speak.

BULLINGBROOK Intended or committed was this fault?
    If on the first, how heinous e'er it be
    To win thy after love I pardon thee.

AUMERLE Then give me leave that I may turn the key   35
    That no man enter till my tale be done.

BULLINGBROOK Have thy desire.

        The Duke of YORK *knocks at the door and crieth.*

YORK [*Within*] My liege, beware, look to thyself.
    Thou hast a traitor in thy presence there.

BULLINGBROOK Villain, I'll make thee safe.   40
        [*Draws his sword.*]

AUMERLE Stay thy revengeful hand. Thou hast no cause to fear.

YORK [*Within*] Open the door, secure foolhardy king.
    Shall I for love speak treason to thy face?
    Open the door or I will break it open!

        Enter YORK.

BULLINGBROOK What is the matter, uncle? Speak.   45
    Recover breath. Tell us how near is danger,
    That we may arm us to encounter it.

YORK Peruse this writing here and thou shalt know
    The treason that my haste forbids me show.

AUMERLE Remember, as thou read'st, thy promise past.   50
    I do repent me. Read not my name there.
    My heart is not confederate with my hand.

YORK It was, villain, ere thy hand did set it down.
    I tore it from the traitor's bosom, king.
    Fear and not love begets his penitence.   55
    Forget to pity him, lest thy pity prove
    A serpent that will sting thee to the heart.

King Henry, as a reward for York's loyalty, is prepared to forgive Aumerle but York will not accept this. The duchess enters to plead for her son's life.

---

1 'Oh loyal father of a treacherous son!'
(in groups of three)

Lines 58–72 emphasise the contrast (antithesis) between father and son. Two of you be Bullingbrook and York, the other the silent Aumerle. Read these lines, pointing clearly to the appropriate person at each contrasting word (father: son, thou: he and so on). Change roles and do it again. Which image shows up the contrast between the two men?

Change roles a third time and present this section highlighting:

a Bullingbrook's horror at Aumerle's treachery and approval of York's loyalty

b York's anguish at the disloyalty of his own son.

2 'What is honour?'

Falstaff, one of Prince Hal's 'unrestrained loose companions' in *Henry IV Part 1*, asks this question just before the Battle of Shrewsbury between Henry IV and his former supporters, Percy (Hotspur) and Worcester (Northumberland had treacherously failed to support his son). Read York's lines about honour (lines 66–72). Mowbray and Bullingbrook speak of it (1.1.175–95), as do Aumerle and the other nobles (4.1.19–85). What is your opinion of these men's concept of honour?

3 Is this tragedy or farce?

Find the line or lines which suggest that King Henry finds the events in this scene somewhat amusing.

---

heinous hateful, infamous (see 4.1.131. Who is right?)
sheer pure
digressing wayward
bawd a woman who procures prostitutes for men

The Beggar . . . King popular Elizabethan ballad
the rest rest sound the rest of the body will remain healthy
confound ruin
dugs breasts

BULLINGBROOK Oh heinous, strong and bold conspiracy!
    Oh loyal father of a treacherous son!
    Thou sheer, immaculate and silver fountain,   60
    From whence this stream through muddy passages
    Hath held his current and defiled himself,
    Thy overflow of good converts to bad,
    And thy abundant goodness shall excuse
    This deadly blot in thy digressing son.   65
YORK So shall my virtue be his vice's bawd
    And he shall spend mine honour with his shame,
    As thriftless sons their scraping fathers' gold.
    Mine honour lives when his dishonour dies,
    Or my shamed life in his dishonour lies.   70
    Thou kill'st me in his life. Giving him breath
    The traitor lives, the true man's put to death.
DUCHESS [*Within*] What ho, my liege! For God's sake let me in!
BULLINGBROOK What shrill-voiced suppliant makes this eager cry?
DUCHESS [*Within*] A woman and thy aunt, great king. 'Tis I.   75
    Speak with me, pity me, open the door!
    A beggar begs that never begged before.
BULLINGBROOK Our scene is altered from a serious thing,
    And now changed to 'The Beggar and the King'.
    My dangerous cousin, let your mother in.   80
    I know she's come to pray for your foul sin.
YORK If thou do pardon whosoever pray,
    More sins for this forgiveness prosper may.
    This festered joint cut off, the rest rest sound.
    This let alone will all the rest confound.   85

Enter DUCHESS.

DUCHESS Oh king, believe not this hard-hearted man.
    Love loving not itself none other can.
YORK Thou frantic woman, what dost thou make here?
    Shall thy old dugs once more a traitor rear?
DUCHESS Sweet York, be patient. Hear me, gentle liege. [*Kneels.*]   90
BULLINGBROOK Rise up, good aunt.
DUCHESS   Not yet, I thee beseech.

The duchess and Aumerle, on their knees, beg King Henry for pardon.
York, also on his knees, demands that his son be punished.

---

1 On your knees (in groups of four)

In a play full of kneelings we now have an abundance of them. Block the movements for lines 86–145. Think carefully about where you direct your lines. A slow and measured first reading with the duchess in particular clearly 'pointing' her lines will help.

Try it in two ways:

a First play it as seriously as you can – Aumerle certainly is not laughing.

b Then play it for comedy – the king certainly seems to find it amusing.

2 A director's problem

Some directors have cut this scene out. Why should they have felt unhappy about it? Can you make a case for keeping it in?

3 Last thoughts on Aumerle and York (in small groups)

This is the last we see of Aumerle and it is the last time that York speaks. There are nineteen scenes in the whole play. To see just how close to events the two men have been, count how many of those nineteen scenes contain one or both men.

Talk together about the parts Aumerle and York have played in these great events. Do you find them sympathetic, comic, tragic? Write down six words to describe the character of each man.

Rutland why does she not call him Aumerle as she did in the previous scene?
and if if
pardonne moy French for 'excuse me, forgive me for refusing you'

sets the word . . . word makes the word contradict itself (as with 'pardon')
chopping French French which twists and changes the meanings of words
sue seek
suit plea (or suit of cards)

For ever will I walk upon my knees
And never see day that the happy sees
Till thou give joy, until thou bid me joy
By pardoning Rutland, my transgressing boy.   95
AUMERLE Unto my mother's prayers I bend my knee. [*Kneels.*]
YORK Against them both my true joints bended be. [*Kneels.*]
    Ill mayst thou thrive if thou grant any grace.
DUCHESS Pleads he in earnest? Look upon his face.
    His eyes do drop no tears, his prayers are in jest,   100
    His words come from his mouth, ours from our breast.
    He prays but faintly, and would be denied.
    We pray with heart and soul and all beside.
    His weary joints would gladly rise, I know.
    Our knees still kneel till to the ground they grow.   105
    His prayers are full of false hypocrisy,
    Ours of true zeal and deep integrity.
    Our prayers do outpray his – then let them have
    That mercy which true prayer ought to have.
BULLINGBROOK Good aunt, stand up.
DUCHESS   Nay, do not say 'stand up',   110
    Say 'pardon' first, and afterwards 'stand up'.
    And if I were thy nurse thy tongue to teach
    'Pardon' should be the first word of thy speech.
    I never longed to hear a word till now.
    Say 'pardon', king. Let pity teach thee how.   115
    The word is short, but not so short as sweet.
    No word like 'pardon' for kings' mouths so meet.
YORK Speak it in French, king. Say 'pardonne moy'.
DUCHESS Dost thou teach pardon pardon to destroy?
    Ah, my sour husband, my hard-hearted lord,   120
    That sets the word itself against the word,
    Speak 'pardon' as 'tis current in our land.
    The chopping French we do not understand.
    Thine eye begins to speak – set thy tongue there,
    Or in thy piteous heart plant thou thine ear   125
    That, hearing how our plaints and prayers do pierce,
    Pity may move thee 'pardon' to rehearse.
BULLINGBROOK Good aunt, stand up.
DUCHESS   I do not sue to stand.
    Pardon is all the suit I have in hand.

King Henry pardons Aumerle but tells York to see to it that the other conspirators are caught and executed. Meanwhile, Exton makes plans to kill King Richard.

1 The role of women in the play (in small groups)

There are only three female characters in the play (excluding the Queen's ladies-in-waiting). Talk about the role the Duchess of York plays in 5.2 and 5.3. Compare her role with the other two women – the queen (2.1, 2.2, 3.4 and 5.1) and the Duchess of Gloucester (1.2).

Women play a much more extensive part in other Shakespeare plays, so why is it that they play such a marginal role in *King Richard II*? Shakespeare obviously developed the role of the queen as he wished (the historical Queen Isabella was barely eleven years old at this time) and could no doubt have developed others.

'Hot seat' the author (i.e. one person steps into the role of Shakespeare and the others ask him questions on the role of women in his play).

2 'A god on earth thou art'

Compare this remark with Mowbray's greeting to the king (1.1.22–4) and Bullingbrook's response to Richard's reduction of the term of his banishment (1.3.212–14). Think about the effect on King Richard of 'the power of the king's word' and the delusions it encouraged. Do you think Bullingbrook is going the same way?

3 Richard's death is plotted (in pairs)

The conspiracy to kill Bullingbrook at Oxford sealed Richard's fate. He was now too dangerous to live. Rehearse a presentation of Scene 4 (it is short enough to be memorised entirely). Present it in the most dramatic way you can. Might this have been the way Richard ordered the death of Gloucester? If indeed he did order it!

---

pardon twain pardon two people, or split the pardon in two
trusty brother-in-law the Duke of Exeter
the abbot Abbot of Westminster (4.1.320–33)

consorted crew gang of associates
prove you true may you prove true, you must prove true
my old son (i.e. the disloyal one that must be made 'new')

BULLINGBROOK I pardon him, as God shall pardon me.   130
DUCHESS Oh happy vantage of a kneeling knee!
       Yet am I sick for fear. Speak it again.
       Twice saying 'pardon' doth not pardon twain,
       But makes one pardon strong.
BULLINGBROOK   With all my heart
       I pardon him.
DUCHESS   A god on earth thou art.   135
BULLINGBROOK But for our trusty brother-in-law and the abbot,
       With all the rest of that consorted crew,
       Destruction straight shall dog them at the heels.
       Good uncle, help to order several powers
       To Oxford or where'er these traitors are.   140
       They shall not live within this world, I swear,
       But I will have them if I once know where.
       Uncle, farewell, and cousin too adieu.
       Your mother well hath prayed, and prove you true.
DUCHESS Come, my old son. I pray God make thee new.   145

                             Exeunt

ACT 5   SCENE 4
Windsor Castle

Enter EXTON and SERVANTS

EXTON Didst thou not mark the king, what words he spake?
       'Have I no friend will rid me of this living fear?'
       Was it not so?
SERVANT   These were his very words.
EXTON 'Have I no friend?' quoth he. He spake it twice,
       And urged it twice together, did he not?   5
SERVANT He did.
EXTON And speaking it, he wishtly looked on me
       As who should say 'I would thou wert the man
       That would divorce this terror from my heart',
       Meaning the king at Pomfret. Come, let's go.   10
       I am the king's friend, and will rid his foe.

                             Exeunt

Richard, the king 'not born to sue but to command' is finally alone.
He peoples the little world of his prison with thoughts.

Richard's costume and pose here are strikingly similar to religious paintings
of Christ before his crucifixion. Find the lines in 4.1 which may have
suggested this parallel.

for because because, since
still breeding ever multiplying
humours temperaments or types
scruples doubts
do set the word . . . word and
  compare contradictory sayings
  from the Bible (see also page 168)
postern small gate

camel . . . needle like Richard,
  scholars then and now have
  puzzled over the different
  meanings of this
for they because they
silly simple-minded
refuge . . . that comfort themselves
  in their disgrace by the thought that

ACT 5   SCENE 5
A prison at Pomfret Castle

Enter RICHARD alone

RICHARD I have been studying how I may compare
   This prison where I live unto the world,
   And for because the world is populous
   And here is not a creature but myself
   I cannot do it. Yet I'll hammer't out.   5
   My brain I'll prove the female to my soul,
   My soul the father, and these two beget
   A generation of still breeding thoughts,
   And these same thoughts people this little world
   In humours like the people of this world,   10
   For no thought is contented. The better sort,
   As thoughts of things divine, are intermixed
   With scruples, and do set the word itself
   Against the word –
   As thus: 'Come, little ones', and then again   15
   'It is as hard to come as for a camel
   To thread the postern of a small needle's eye.'
   Thoughts tending to ambition, they do plot
   Unlikely wonders: how these vain weak nails
   May tear a passage through the flinty ribs   20
   Of this hard world my ragged prison walls,
   And, for they cannot, die in their own pride.
   Thoughts tending to content flatter themselves
   That they are not the first of Fortune's slaves,
   Nor shall not be the last, like silly beggars   25
   Who, sitting in the stocks, refuge their shame
   That many have and others must set there,
   And in this thought they find a kind of ease,
   Bearing their own misfortunes on the back
   Of such as have before endured the like.   30

Only the thought of ceasing to exist offers Richard any hope of relief.
He hears music and his mind dwells on the mystery of time.

---

1 Follow Richard's thoughts (in groups of four)

Richard explores his own fall. Read lines 1–66 together, taking a line or two each. You will need to do this more than once. Try to express in your voice the contrasts between, for example, 'this prison' and 'the world', 'king' and 'beggar' and so on. Count each item in the various lists that he makes. When you have done this, write down a list of the different things that Richard's mind dwells on. Can you as a group, use the words you have collected to create your own dramatic picture of Richard's inner world?

2 'My state and time' (in pairs)

Music is played to comfort Richard (line 41), but the musician fumbles and cannot keep the rhythm. Read lines 41–8, taking a sentence each. How does the music Richard hears remind him of the follies of his own life?

Then read lines 49–60 taking a sentence each. In an elaborate comparison (or conceit) Richard imagines how time has turned him into a clock. **Conceits** are images worked out carefully and in great detail (Richard says himself that he will 'hammer it out' in line 5). List all the time (or clock) words and next to each write the thing that Richard compares them to (for example: 'minutes = thoughts').

Richard uses another conceit in lines 1–30, where he imagines his thoughts filling the prison cell just as people fill the world outside.

What is it in lines 61–6 that brings Richard's soliloquy to an end?

---

penury poverty
ha, ha not a laugh – what then?
proportion rhythm or beat
numbering clock clock with a face
  that tells the hours and minutes
jar tick, move

watches time intervals
outward watch clock-face
Jack of the clock figure which
  strikes the bell
holp helped
strange brooch rare jewel

Thus play I in one person many people,
And none contented. Sometimes am I king,
Then treasons make me wish myself a beggar,
And so I am. Then crushing penury
Persuades me I was better when a king,   35
Then am I kinged again, and by and by
Think that I am unkinged by Bullingbrook,
And straight am nothing. But whate'er I be
Nor I nor any man that but man is
With nothing shall be pleased till he be eased   40
With being nothing.
                    The music plays.
                    Music do I hear?
Ha, ha, keep time! How sour sweet music is
When time is broke and no proportion kept.
So is it in the music of men's lives.
And here have I the daintiness of ear   45
To check time broke in a disordered string,
But for the concord of my state and time
Had not an ear to hear my true time broke.
I wasted time and now doth time waste me,
For now hath time made me his numbering clock.   50
My thoughts are minutes, and with sighs they jar
Their watches on unto mine eyes, the outward watch,
Whereto my finger like a dial's point
Is pointing still, in cleansing them from tears.
Now sir, the sound that tells what hour it is   55
Are clamorous groans that strike upon my heart,
Which is the bell. So sighs and tears and groans
Show minutes, times and hours. But my time
Runs posting on in Bullingbrook's proud joy
While I stand fooling here, his Jack of the clock.   60
This music mads me. Let it sound no more,
For though it have holp madmen to their wits
In me it seems it will make wise men mad.
Yet blessing on his heart that gives it me,
For 'tis a sign of love, and love to Richard   65
Is a strange brooch in this all-hating world.

Richard is visited by one of the grooms from his stables.

---

1 'Hail, royal prince!' (in groups of four to six)

Whatever else he may have lost, Richard still has his quickness of mind. Compare the way he responds here to the groom's greeting with the way he responded to Mowbray and Bullingbrook's greetings in the opening scene (1.1.25–7). A 'royal' and a 'noble' were coins. Two royals were equivalent to a pound sterling, as were three nobles. So therefore ten groats (another coin) was the difference in value between a royal and a noble.

Show how far Richard has come since the opening of the play. Two of you read lines 67–94, pausing frequently. The others echo, in those pauses, appropriate lines and phrases taken from 1.1 and 1.3. This will take a little time to prepare and rehearse.

2 Loyalty again (in pairs)

Ironically, the groom's attempts at comforting Richard by talking of his horse cause Richard considerable pain. Sit facing your partner and read this page taking a part each. How would you describe the groom's kind of loyalty?

3 Realisation

Several times in Acts 3 and 4 Richard expressed a longing to give up the cares and responsibilities of kingship. Now he realises the consequences of losing power. Read lines 92–4 several times then close your eyes and visualise the image the words call up.

---

sometime former
erned grieved
roan of mixed colour
Barbary a fine breed of horse but also here the actual name

jade worthless horse (see 3.3.179)
clapping him patting him
burthen burden
galled chafed
jauncing prancing, bouncing

GROOM Hail, royal prince!

RICHARD   Thanks, noble peer.
    The cheapest of us is ten groats too dear.
    What art thou? And how comest thou hither
    Where no man never comes but that sad dog   7c
    That brings me food to make misfortune live?

GROOM I was a poor groom of thy stable, king,
    When thou wert king, who, travelling towards York,
    With much ado at length have gotten leave
    To look upon my sometime royal master's face.   75
    Oh, how it erned my heart when I beheld
    In London streets that coronation day
    When Bullingbrook rode on roan Barbary,
    That horse that thou so often hast bestrid,
    That horse that I so carefully have dressed.   8c

RICHARD Rode he on Barbary? Tell me, gentle friend,
    How went he under him?

GROOM So proudly as if he disdained the ground.

RICHARD So proud that Bullingbrook was on his back.
    That jade hath ate bread from my royal hand,   85
    This hand hath made him proud with clapping him.
    Would he not stumble, would he not fall down,
    Since pride must have a fall, and break the neck
    Of that proud man that did usurp his back?
    Forgiveness! Horse, why do I rail on thee,   9c
    Since thou, created to be awed by man,
    Wast born to bear? I was not made a horse
    And yet I bear a burthen like an ass,
    Spurred, galled and tired by jauncing Bullingbrook.

Richard suspects that his food is poisoned and attacks his jailer, whereupon Exton and his men enter. Richard fights bravely, killing several of them, before Exton strikes him down.

1 What kind of death? (in groups of six)

For the Elizabethans, the killing of a king was a devastating crime. Read lines 95–118 and then write notes on the moves and actions required here. Although there have been many confrontations in the rest of the play, this is the only fight scene. Note particularly lines 106 and 118. Holinshed records one account of Richard's death which has him strike the keeper on the head with the carving knife, then seize a pike from one of his attackers and kill four men before being killed himself. Can you work out how many men Shakespeare makes him kill? Rehearse a dumb show presentation of this section using your blocking notes and see what kind of death your version creates.

2 The birth of a legend (in pairs)

In line 110, Richard certainly still regards himself as the true king. Indeed, after his death, he came to be revered as the 'martyr king'. Read the last words of Richard and Exton (lines 108–18) very slowly, 'pointing' and gesturing at every possible word. Do you feel that a legend is being born?

3 Why this death?

Holinshed offered two other versions of Richard's death besides the Exton story. He possibly died of starvation or starved himself to death. Consider why Shakespeare should have chosen the Exton version. You may have further ideas when you get to the final scene of the play!

4 The groom's story

Tell your family the story of your visit to the deposed king.

---

meat food
fall to begin eating
this rude assault this vicious
  attack

Enter KEEPER *to Richard with meat.*

KEEPER Fellow, give place. Here is no longer stay.   95
RICHARD If thou love me 'tis time thou wert away.
GROOM What my tongue dares not, that my heart shall say.   *Exit*
KEEPER My lord, wilt please you to fall to?
RICHARD Taste of it first as thou art wont to do.
KEEPER My lord, I dare not. Sir Pierce of Exton,   100
  Who lately came from the king, commands the contrary.
RICHARD The devil take Henry of Lancaster, and thee!
  Patience is stale, and I am weary of it!
    [*Beats the Keeper.*]
KEEPER Help, help, help!

  The murderers [EXTON *and Servants*] *rush in.*

RICHARD How now! What means death in this rude assault?   105
  Villain, thy own hand yields thy death's instrument.
  Go thou and fill another room in hell.
    Here Exton strikes him down.

  That hand shall burn in never-quenching fire
  That staggers thus my person. Exton, thy fierce hand
  Hath with the king's blood stained the king's own land.   110
  Mount, mount my soul. Thy seat is up on high
  Whilst my gross flesh sinks downward, here to die. [*Dies.*]
EXTON As full of valour as of royal blood.
  Both have I spilled. Oh, would the deed were good,
  For now the devil that told me I did well   115
  Says that this deed is chronicled in hell.
  This dead king to the living king I'll bear.
  Take hence the rest and give them burial here.
           Exeunt

Bullingbrook hears news of the execution of the rebel leaders.
Percy brings in the Bishop of Carlisle for judgement.

---

1 Mirror image (in groups of five to seven)

There are strange echoes of the opening scene in these final moments of the play. Where King Richard first appeared with his aged counsellor Gaunt, now King Henry appears with Gaunt's brother York. Later, the dead Richard is granted the respect and ceremony reminiscent of his first entrance.

Read this scene through together and talk about the ways in which it is similar yet strangely different to the opening scene. Think about the stage picture as well as the words and images that the characters use.

Then block the moves for lines 1–29, using the same kinds of ceremonial kneelings and bowings as you did for the opening scene. Do you sense a different atmosphere?

2 Northumberland and Percy

Are these two men, who have been so instrumental in securing the crown for Bullingbrook, already becoming lukewarm in their support of King Henry?

3 Dealing with rebels

Count the number of severed heads mentioned in this scene. How many heads in total has Henry Bullingbrook now cut off? This particular batch of heads was set on poles over London Bridge 'to the terror of others'.

---

the rebels the members of the Abbot's conspiracy
Ciceter Cirencester
Kent the demoted Duke of Surrey who supported Aumerle in 4.1.60–71

at large discoursèd related in full
consorted conspiring
I wot I know
clog wooden weight used to keep animals from straying
doom judgement, punishment

ACT 5   SCENE 6
Windsor Castle

Flourish. Enter BULLINGBROOK, YORK, *with other Lords and attendants*

BULLINGBROOK Kind uncle York, the latest news we hear
Is that the rebels have consumed with fire
Our town of Ciceter in Gloucestershire,
But whether they be ta'en or slain we hear not.

Enter NORTHUMBERLAND.

Welcome, my lord. What is the news?   5
NORTHUMBERLAND First, to thy sacred state wish I all happiness.
The next news is I have to London sent
The heads of Salisbury, Spencer, Blunt and Kent.
The manner of their taking may appear
At large discoursèd in this paper here.   10
BULLINGBROOK We thank thee, gentle Percy, for thy pains,
And to thy worth will add right worthy gains.

Enter Lord FITZWATER.

FITZWATER My lord, I have from Oxford sent to London
The heads of Broccas and Sir Bennet Seely,
Two of the dangerous consorted traitors   15
That sought at Oxford thy dire overthrow.
BULLINGBROOK Thy pains, Fitzwater, shall not be forgot.
Right noble is thy merit, well I wot.

Enter PERCY *and* CARLISLE.

PERCY The grand conspirator, Abbot of Westminster,
With clog of conscience and sour melancholy   20
Hath yielded up his body to the grave.
But here is Carlisle living, to abide
Thy kingly doom and sentence of his pride.

Henry pardons Carlisle and is then confronted with the body of Richard.
He condemns Exton's actions and promises a pilgrimage to the Holy Land
to atone for the killing.

1 Final picture (in groups of eight)
Create a tableau of the entrance of Exton with the body of Richard.

2 Final images
a Blood
Find the blood images in this final section and link them back to
some of the other blood images that you recall in the rest of the
play (start with 1.1.51).

b Repentance
This is the third time Bullingbrook has mentioned a pilgrimage
(lines 49–50). Read the opening of *Henry IV Part 1* to see if he
keeps his promise.

c Guilt
'With Cain go wander through the shades of night' says
Bullingbrook as he dismisses Exton. Find a similar phrase in the
opening scene which Bullingbrook uses against Mowbray (and
thus indirectly against Richard). In what sense is Bullingbrook now
guilty of the same crime as Richard?

3 Final words (in pairs)
Bullingbrook made the first major speech in the play and here he
makes the last. Read it to each other and ask yourselves if you believe
him. Did you believe him in 1.1?

---

reverend room place of religious
  retirement
more than thou hast possibly
  'more spacious than the prison you
  have been in'

with Cain see the Bible Genesis 4,
  verses 8–16
incontinent immediately

BULLINGBROOK Carlisle, this is your doom:
      Choose out some secret place, some reverend room,   25
      More than thou hast, and with it joy thy life.
      So, as thou livest in peace die free from strife.
      For though mine enemy thou hast ever been
      High sparks of honour in thee have I seen.

Enter EXTON *with a coffin.*

EXTON Great king, within this coffin I present   30
      Thy buried fear. Herein all breathless lies
      The mightiest of thy greatest enemies,
      Richard of Bordeaux, by me hither brought.
BULLINGBROOK Exton, I thank thee not, for thou hast wrought
      A deed of slander with thy fatal hand   35
      Upon my head and all this famous land.
EXTON From your own mouth, my lord, did I this deed.
BULLINGBROOK They love not poison that do poison need.
      Nor do I thee. Though I did wish him dead,
      I hate the murderer, love him murderèd.   40
      The guilt of conscience take thou for thy labour,
      But neither my good word nor princely favour.
      With Cain go wander through shades of night
      And never show thy head by day nor light.
      Lords, I protest my soul is full of woe   45
      That blood should sprinkle me to make me grow.
      Come mourn with me for what I do lament,
      And put on sullen black incontinent.
      I'll make a voyage to the Holy Land
      To wash this blood off from my guilty hand.   50
      March sadly after. Grace my mournings here
      In weeping after this untimely bier.
                              Exeunt

Looking back at the play

1 Double vision (in large groups)

How strong is your sense of the 'double nature' of *King Richard II*? Present a 'parallel play', a simultaneous dramatisation of the 'double events' of Act 5, the final moments in the twin journeys of the two royal cousins. Your play could perhaps switch suddenly from king to king, or two scenes could be shown together. Freeze frames, dumb shows or echoes have possibilities. Or you could 'inter-cut' (i.e. select lines, phrases or events from one part of Act 5 and use them in another).

2 Write King Richard's obituary

You are the obituaries editor for a national newspaper. Write King Richard's obituary in as fair and accurate a fashion as you can. Talk about his personal qualities as well as his political career.

3 Put King Henry on trial

A fresh rebellion has dethroned Henry. Conduct his trial as if it were in a modern court room. You will need people to be the prosecution team, the defence team plus others to act as witnesses.

This activity will need time to prepare. All groups need to study the relevant scenes and make notes. The prosecution and defence will need to prepare their questions, plan their cross-examinations and come to an agreement as to which witnesses will be called. The witnesses will be characters from the play acting in role. Remember that only evidence from the play is admissible, although you may include hearsay evidence (i.e. what someone says).

4 'Because we thought ourself thy lawful king'

This is how Richard addresses Northumberland just before his crucial meeting with Bullingbrook at Flint Castle (3.3.74), using the royal pronoun (the 'royal we') as he has done many times in the play for public pronouncements. Whereabouts does Richard abandon this usage and where does Bullingbrook first take it up for himself?

5 A modern stage set

You were asked to visualise the opening scene as it might have been performed on an Elizabethan stage. Below is a picture of the stage set for the 1986 RSC production.

a The sun emblem moved from left to right over the zodiacal arch to match Richard's personal career. Decide on your positions for it.

b The two carved and sculptured stone thrones were moved around the stage like giant chess-pieces as events unfolded. Decide the position of these thrones for 1.2, 2.1 and 5.2.

c The central pillar could be raised fully, half-raised with steps placed in front of it, or lowered completely to the floor. The open sides to the column could be filled with trellis work or prison bars. Decide how you would use this central column for 1.1, 3.3, 4.1, 5.5.

At the end of the performance, the central pillar suddenly revolved. It revealed a profusion of red and white climbing roses. In the background, the gardeners sharpening their scythes suddenly looked like the grim reapers of Time. In these two stage pictures, the audience was made uneasily aware of the civil discord of the 'Wars of the Roses' and of the future troubled reign of Henry IV.

Perspectives

The purpose of the following pages is to get you to look at the play from a variety of perspectives, or viewpoints. Bushy uses the word **perspectives** in Act 2:

> . . . 'sorrow's eye, glazèd with blinding tears,
> Divides one thing entire to many objects,
> Like perspectives, which rightly gazed upon
> Show nothing but confusion; eyed awry
> Distinguish form.'   2.2.16–20

'Perspectives' were paintings which were apparently distorted when viewed from the front, but which appeared regular and properly proportioned when viewed from an angle.

The long greyish mark twisted slantwise across the centre bottom of Holbein's *The Ambassadors* (page 64) appears compressed by perspective when viewed from an acute angle, so that the viewer sees the vivid image of a human skull. The painting was originally hung so that as the viewer came up the staircase the angle ensured that only the image of the skull appeared. As the viewer came level with the picture, the image of the skull was lost and the main body of the picture became visible. As he continued, the main picture faded to reveal the skull image again.

The portrait of Edward VI (1546) is another perspective. In Shakespeare's time it was shown to every tourist visiting Whitehall Palace. Viewed 'rightly' (from the front) the king's face appeared grotesquely distorted. When viewed 'awry' (obliquely) through a special viewing device attached to the frame, the king's head could be seen in proper proportion.

Another popular Elizabethan perspective was a 'multiplying glass'. This was a glass cut into a number of facets, each of which created a distinct image as you looked through it.

When Bushy (2.2.14–27) attempts to console the queen, he says that simple sorrow has distorted her judgement and made her mind look 'awry' upon a perfectly normal event, as if it were some ingenious trick picture (or 'perspective') hiding more terrible fears. Yet as Bushy speaks, his words shift and change their meanings as if they too were taking on some of the qualities of these strange perspective pictures. At one moment he seems to be saying that the queen's tears have blurred ('glazed') the image of the world she sees as if she were looking through a perspective glass (2.2.16–7). Then the next moment he seems to be saying that she sees imaginary fears because she does not look 'rightly' at the world, just as people see new images ('distinguish form') when they look 'awry' at a perspective picture (2.2.19–20).

As you read Bushy's words, keep that sensation of shifting images in your mind, because the whole play is full of shifting and contradictory meanings and viewpoints. We are in a world where certainty and clarity are breaking down. The line of kings which had ruled England by undisputed right of succession since the time of William the Conqueror is coming to an end. If Richard is deposed, what can words like 'royalty' or 'loyalty' now mean?

Remember that just as there is no one image, so there is no one meaning to the play. Events are seen from multiple points of view. By the time we reach Act 2 Scene 2 we have already seen Gaunt, York, Northumberland and the queen present their particular view of events, and there are several other centres of sympathy in the play, notably King Richard himself in the later acts. Perhaps what Shakespeare is saying is that trying to make sense of the world is rather like viewing a 'perspective' and that we are by our very nature unable to perceive the entire truth, especially the truth of history.

King Richard II as theatre

There has been a significant change in the way the play has been viewed over the centuries.

The play in Elizabethan times

The competence and safety of the monarch was of the greatest importance to the Elizabethans. The fate of England itself depended on it. The political and constitutional issues raised in the play were, therefore, of paramount importance. This was so sensitive a subject that when the play was first printed, the deposition scene (4.1.154–319) was censored, and only restored after Queen Elizabeth's death. The queen knew that people likened her to Richard II. Like him, she was childless and there were disputes over her succession. Like him, she was accused of having favourites and wasting money.

We know very little about how particular plays were performed in Elizabethan times. Even so, knowing the politically sensitive nature of *King Richard II*, it is tempting to think that Shakespeare's company might have presented Richard as a sympathetic martyr deposed by a shady and unscrupulous Bullingbrook. However, when the followers of the Earl of Essex ordered a performance of the play on the eve of their ill-fated rebellion against Elizabeth, Shakespeare's company might well have felt obliged to present Bullingbrook as a rather more charismatic figure!

The play in the nineteenth century

During the eighteenth century, as the monarchy lost its central place in the British political system, so interest in the play shifted. By the nineteenth and early twentieth centuries, the play was seen as the personal tragedy of Richard.

Some twentieth-century interpretations

John Gielgud saw the language of the play as creating a 'beautiful, tapestried, somewhat Gothic effect, like an illuminated missal or a Book of Hours ... Everyone speaks in images, parentheses and elaborate similes'. Gielgud's Richard was a kind of poet, a man keenly aware of his own ability to weave words together.

John Barton's 1973 Royal Shakespeare Company production emphasised the 'doubleness' of the play. Both Richard and Bullingbrook were made up to resemble each other (see page 136), but Richard was dressed in white while Bullingbrook and his followers were dressed in black, thus emphasising the fundamental opposition between them. They even looked at each other at one point through the broken frame of the mirror, as if to make the point that they were identical yet opposite. This doubleness was heightened by having the two actors playing Richard and Bullingbrook alternate playing the two central roles on different nights.

The 1986 RSC production presented the two major protagonists in a rather different way. It was set in a brightly-coloured, ordered and secure medieval garden, with King Richard the brightest and most elegant of jewels. Into this world strode a quite amazing Bullingbrook, who made it absolutely clear from the start that he was a man after big game. A man of 'restless arrogance', he was described by one critic as 'spitting and lurching through the play like a lizard scampering in a hot climate' (see pages 138 and 142), creating a sense in the opening scenes that here was a real power struggle.

The 1988 Phoenix Theatre production showed a harsh, dark, metallic England. In the early scenes, Richard was played as a callous even brutish tyrant who believed he was rendered all-powerful by the mystic power of kingship and who shocked even his own courtiers by the blow he aimed at the dying Gaunt. Yet amazingly, this tyrant took on a dignity and grace as he rid himself of the trappings of kingship. At the end there was sympathy, too, for Bullingbrook. As the lights dimmed on the new king throned on high, Henry stared into the hollow circle of his crown and emitted an equally hollow laugh.

1 See a production of *King Richard II*

There is no substitute for seeing a live production. Shakespeare and his company were selling 'a heard-and-seen experience'. Many of the things mentioned below are worth keeping in mind as you watch the play.

2 Director's notes for a new production

Read the play through as if you have been given a chance to direct it. Keep a systematic record of your thoughts, but do not get bogged down with small details. Bear in mind the following points:

• Shakespeare's 'internal stage directions'. Be sensitive to what the words are making visible (atmosphere, place, gesture, character).

- Work out the shape and sweep of a scene, how scenes echo and contrast with each other. In particular, work out how the big scenes should be staged and their changes of mood, pattern and pace.
- Watch how characters come into being, how they grow and change with each appearance (Richard and Bullingbrook, obviously, but also characters like York and Aumerle). Remember the 'silent watchers'. Characters are always in action or responding to others' actions.
- Think about the kind of language each character uses, the swings of emotion in big scenes, the movement of thoughts in long speeches. Occasionally pick out a line at random and decide how you want that actor/actress to speak it.
- Watch for the echoes, parallels and links through which the themes develop.
- Write notes for your stage designer/costume designer.

3 Preparing a role

A good way to approach the study of a character is to imagine that you are preparing to act that role yourself.

You could:

- Make notes on how you think your character should be played in each scene in which they appear.
- Collect examples of your character's language.
- Actions reveal character. Make a list of what your character actually does throughout the play.
- Explore a character's motives. 'Hot seat' your character. One person takes on the role. Others question or probe his/her motives and actions in the play.

King Richard II as political history

It may surprise you to know that both Henry IV and the Tudor monarchs pursued policies very similar to Richard II in their dealings with the nobility. Looked at from a historical perspective, the play is no longer peopled with strangely colourful kings and knights but with powerful men facing difficult political and economic problems.

The relationship between king and nobles

Within the feudal system, the balance of power between crown and nobles was inherently unstable. Only with a strong and effective king could there be peace in the realm, but the stronger the king became the more uneasy and hostile the nobles became, since they regarded it as their natural right to share in the government of the country.

How powerful was the king?

Monarchs bolstered their authority by promoting the idea of 'Divine Right'. They were the 'Lord's anointed'. The historical Richard certainly believed that God had appointed him to rule the people. In reality, however, the king was not all-powerful. His Coronation Oath required him to promise to govern according to the law. Custom and law must stand even above the king.

In any case, no feudal king had sufficient money or military power to defy completely the desires of the more powerful lords. To rule effectively a king had to lead his barons and persuade the Great Council (or Parliament as it was increasingly being called) that his was the right way. Richard was by no means the first or the last English king to be plagued by unruly barons.

Were Edward III and the Black Prince really so wonderful?

Waging a foreign war kept the war-like barons happy and their private armies occupied. The initial successes of Richard's father and grandfather in France (at Poitiers and Crécy) were spectacular, but the war drained the country's resources so that, at his death, Edward III had lost virtually all the territory he had gained in France. Richard therefore tried a policy of peace with France, which was economically sensible but which angered and disappointed the nobles. The temptation for them to use their private armies, now hardened in battle, must have been enormous.

Were Edward III and his sons really so close?

The love between Edward III and his family seems to have been genuine enough, particularly between the Black Prince (Richard's father) and Gaunt. However, Edward's use of his family to help him govern the country left a legacy for Richard of rich and powerful uncles all of whom assumed it was their right to govern England.

The Most Powerful Family in England

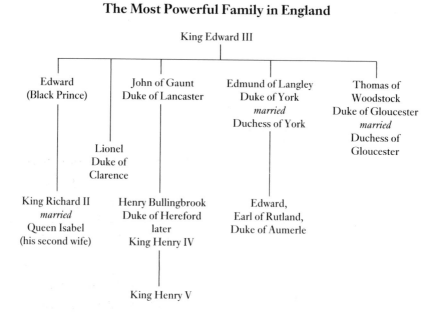

This is a simplified genealogical tree of the Royal Family. Edward III in fact had seven sons, but two died in infancy. All those named here (except Lionel, Duke of Clarence) either feature or are mentioned in the play.

The Tree of Jesse

In the Old Testament, Jesse, the father of David, had seven sons. Medieval pictures and carvings often showed a tree growing from him and culminating in the figure of Christ. Edward III also had seven sons – a coincidence which the duchess uses in 1.2.

In a similar fashion, Elizabethan engravings show the line of succession growing like a tree from Edward III, dividing into the two houses of York and Lancaster (the period of the 'Wars of the Roses'), reuniting in Henry VII and culminating in Elizabeth I.

Did Richard order the death of the Duke of Gloucester?

Holinshed, Shakespeare's major historical source, states that Richard did give the order, but that Mowbray delayed carrying it out for several weeks until the king threatened him with death if he failed to obey. It was a view commonly held in Shakespeare's time that the king *did* order the killing.

The historical Gloucester, however, was by no means a 'plain well-meaning soul' as Gaunt describes him in the play. He was a persistent thorn in the flesh of the king and had staged at least one power coup. He even taunted the king when he was negotiating peace terms with France with these words:

'Sire, you ought first to hazard your life in capturing a city from your enemies before you think of giving up any city which your ancestors have conquered.'

Was Richard a tyrant who brought about his own downfall?

Richard, like many monarchs before him, determined to be his own master, but it was a dangerous business. He needed a large income and a permanent army to overpower the nobles, and was therefore driven to use increasingly dubious methods of raising money. He forced those who had offended him to purchase pardons ('fines'); wealthy individuals who had given support (real or imagined) to the king's enemies had to sign blank documents ('blank charters') which the king could fill in later with whatever amount he chose. The play states that some people were required to make gifts, or rather forced loans ('benevolences'), to the king, but this is not historically correct. Richard did, however, 'farm the realm' (i.e. allocated parts of the country to tax-farmers who paid him money for the right to extort taxes on their own behalf).

The hostility amongst the nobility and wealthy merchant classes was enormous. Men were bewildered and worried and Richard's seizure of Bullingbrook's inheritance was the last straw. It would be fair to say that Richard's behaviour did become erratic and unbalanced in the final years of his reign, but he very nearly managed to gain absolute control over the nobles and might have succeeded had the feudal machinery of government been able to cope.

The scramble for patronage

The king had immense powers of patronage: gifts of land, titles and government positions. It was a powerful weapon and could be used to create loyalty. The court was therefore the centre of the whole political system, a place where men desperately tried to catch the king's favour.

Both Bullingbrook and Mowbray benefited from Richard's patronage, receiving lands and titles. Aumerle gained his dukedom at the expense of the disgraced Lords Appellant, and benefited from the confiscated lands of the dead Duke of Gaunt, as did the Duke of Surrey. Both men lost their dukedoms when Bullingbrook became king. Aumerle reverted to the title of the Earl of Rutland, and Surrey reverted to the Earl of Kent.

The king's favourites

Richard built up support around him by using his powers of patronage to appoint his chosen men to positions in the royal household, and to advance some of the younger nobles who also threw in their lot with him. This naturally enraged the established nobles. There was a certain hypocrisy in these attacks on the king's favourites, because those doing so were very often themselves unscrupulous in furthering their own interests. Yet in a sense it was necessary, for a noble who was not in a position of influence was vulnerable to attacks from those who were.

Bushy, Green and Bagot represented the parliamentary class and gave Richard valuable support in the Commons. They were of the gentry but 'base' (i.e. far lower in the hierarchy than the great lords, who therefore despised them).

Did the real Richard fall or was he pushed?

The Richard of the play seems almost to fall of his own accord. Bullingbrook stumbles across him by chance in Flint Castle (3.3.19–25), whereupon the king capitulates without a struggle. This is almost certainly not historically correct. Holinshed records that Richard was secure in Conway Castle when he was promised safe conduct under oath by Northumberland who then laid an ambush and took him prisoner.

It is also very doubtful whether Richard really agreed to abdicate. The actual 'abdication' took place privately in the Tower of London. Although the official records state that Richard agreed to abdicate and named Bullingbrook as his successor, they were very probably altered and the chroniclers given an official version after the event.

Fiction, fact or 'faction'?

Film and television sometimes create 'faction', the presentation of an actual event which is a mingling of factual truth and imaginative-dramatic truth. *King Richard II* is in a sense a 'faction'. Act 4, for example, never happened exactly as Shakespeare presents it, but neither is it entirely 'untruthful'.

Create your own faction (in play or novel form) based on one of the events leading up to the opening of the play, or on an event referred to by Shakespeare but not actually dramatised (for example, the meeting of the King's Council at Coventry, or Richard and Bullingbrook's entry to London).

How Shakespeare used his sources

Shakespeare's major source is quite clearly Raphael Holinshed's *Chronicles of England, Ireland and Scotland* (1586–7). This history was based on a variety of sources both hostile and favourable to King Richard. Shakespeare must have sensed the possibilities. It would suit his dramatist's sense of tension to present a 'many-sided' picture of King Richard's deposition. He does not follow Holinshed's account slavishly, however.

- He alters events (page 195), changes their order or telescopes them (page 125) and adds new ones (pages 18–21 and 116–23). Gaunt's vision of England, for example, and most of the events surrounding the queen seem to be Shakespeare's additions.
- Characters are changed or developed (for example, Gaunt, Northumberland, the Duchesses of York and Gloucester). The queen was actually only eleven years old at this time. In particular he develops the character of Richard himself.
- He adds symbolic images and actions such as the crown (3.2.160–77), its use as prop in 4.1, the use of mirrors and shadows (4.1.263–301).

Read this brief extract from Holinshed. Then read (or preferably dramatise) 3.3.172–209. Shakespeare has kept closely to the basic sequence of events but see how he has explored the implications behind Holinshed's account.

> 'The earle of Northumberland, returning to the castell, appointed the king to be set to dinner (for he was fasting till then) and, after he had dined, the duke (Bullingbrook) came downe to the castell himselfe, and entred the same all armed, his bassenet onelie excepted; and being within the first gate, he staied there, till the king came foorth of the inner part of the castell unto him.
>
> The king, accompanied with the bishop of Carleill, the earle of Salisburie, and sir Stephan Scroope, knight, (who bare the sword before him,) and a few other, came foorth into the utter [outer] ward, and sate down in a place prepared for him. Foorthwith, as the duke got sight of the king, he shewed a reuerend dutie, as became him, in bowing his knee . . .'

Extract from Holinshed

King Richard II as tragedy

The title of the First Quarto edition of the play was *The Tragedy of King Richard II*. What tragic qualities does the play possess?

The nature of tragedy

There have been many definitions of the term **tragedy** over the centuries. Here are just some of the things that have been said:

- In the Middle Ages, a tragedy was the story of a great historical or legendary character who, by chance, accident or misfortune, fell into humility, poverty and misery. There was always a moral: life is uncertain and we should trust only in the immortality of Heaven.
- Aristotle argued that watching the terrible events of a tragedy aroused the emotions of pity and fear in such a way that the audience was 'purged' or 'healed' (he called it 'catharsis').
- In a tragedy, Fate, Destiny or Divine Providence (a kind of power outside of man) often plays a part in the unfolding of events.
- The tragic hero is a man with weaknesses like our own. Yet, in the face of disaster and suffering (in part self-inflicted), he possesses the strength to endure and the power to apprehend and sympathise. In the tragic hero we hear 'the voice of a man who is really in pain'.
- A tragedy asks fundamental questions about the nature and purpose of existence.

1 Is King Richard a tragic figure?

Judging by the above comments, can you describe Richard as a tragic hero? In particular, think about whether you ever hear in Richard 'the voice of a man who is really in pain'.

2 Compare the play with Shakespeare's 'great' tragedies

Read *Macbeth* and compare the two central figures, Macbeth and Richard. *Macbeth* was also based on Holinshed's Chronicles but the resulting play is very different to *King Richard II*. Alternatively, read *Hamlet*. Some people have seen in Richard an 'embryo Hamlet'.

The tragedy of kingship

Shakespeare wrote eight plays which, when put together, tell the story of English history from Richard II to Henry VII (Elizabeth's grand-father). The three sequel plays to *King Richard II* (*Henry IV Parts 1* and *2* and *Henry V*) show the tragic effects on Henry IV of the burden of kingship which is afterwards taken up by his son, Henry V. This is how a sick and diseased Henry IV looks back on his life in *Henry IV Part 2*:

'O God, that one might read the book of fate,
And see the revolution of the times . . .
                                        . . . O, if this were seen,
The happiest youth, viewing his progress through,
What perils past, what crosses to ensue,
Would shut the book and sit him down and die.'   3.1.45ff

3 'Uneasy lies the head that wears a crown'

These also are King Henry IV's words (*Henry IV Part 2* 3.1.31). Do you sense in the final act of *King Richard II* the same kind of tragic destiny beginning to surround Bullingbrook as had once surrounded Richard?

4 'Mark silent king'

Henry Bullingbrook is a more fully developed character in the *Henry IV* plays. Find the following extracts from the Henry plays and decide if they help to clarify your picture of Bullingbrook as he is seen as "Richard II":

Henry IV Part 1 (3.2.45–84 and 93–9)
Henry IV Part 2 (3.1.5–79)
Henry IV Part 2 (4.5.183–219).

5 The tragedy of the king's two bodies

Some have seen King Richard's tragedy as lying in the dual nature of his existence. The king is in essence a twin-natured being.

One of the ideas that lay behind the 1973 RSC production (page 188) was the Elizabethan doctrine of 'The king's two bodies'. According to this theory, the king is set apart from his subjects by possessing two natures. One of these bodies is flawless, abstract and immortal. The other is fallible, individual and subject to time and decay. These two natures are fused at the moment of coronation in a way that deliberately parallels the incarnation of Christ, whose representative on earth (as Richard in the play reminds us) the king will be from now on.

It is interesting that the process of acting also sets up a dual-natured being. Queen Elizabeth I herself remarked on the similarity between the monarch and the actor:

'We Princes are set on stages, in the sight and view of all the world duly observed. The eyes of many behold our actions.'

Perhaps the play's tragedy can be seen in the conflict between the two roles that first Richard and then Bullingbrook are called upon to assume. In the end, both men pay a high price for taking on these dual roles or twin natures. Richard's journey from king to mere man is balanced by Bullingbrook's journey from a single to a twin-natured being. Both gain and lose enormously. Each story is in its way tragic.

6 'Yet looks he like a king'

In what ways does Richard seem to consciously act the role of king in Acts 1–3? Find examples from Act 3 onwards where Richard and others use acting images to describe his situation and behaviour.

Do you think Bullingbrook's change in behaviour from Act 4 onwards is due to his taking on the new and unfamiliar role of king?

7 Is England itself the tragic hero of the play?

If you look at the heart of the play, namely the garden scene (3.4), yet another image emerges – the image of England itself. Many scenes are very specifically localised (see page 147). Look first at 3.4 and then read Richard's speech after the combat (1.3.125–39), Gaunt's vision of England (2.1.40–66), Richard's speech on his return from Ireland (3.2.4–26) and Carlisle's speech in Westminster Hall (4.1.134–49).

Is it possible to see England itself as the tragic figure in this play?

The language of *King Richard II*

The play, with its symmetrical journeys of the two central characters, is full of images of balance and change, opposition and contradiction. The gardener's scales and Richard's buckets are just two of many.

Elemental imagery

> 'Fire and water struggle for the earth of England and conduct their fight with the airy breath of words.'   (Andrew Gurr)

Many of the images in the play are organised around the four elements: earth, air, fire and water. Medieval and Elizabethan belief was that these elements made up the entire world. Fire and air were upwardly aspiring elements, while earth and water tended downwards. Human character, too, was felt to be a combination of these four elements. The body was washed in random fashion by four fluids or humours (blood, choler, melancholy and phlegm). Each, like the four elements, possessed different combinations of qualities. Blood, like air, was warm and humid, choler, like fire, was hot and dry.

As the play unfolds, the stage picture of Richard throned in state is replaced by Bullingbrook. Likewise, the two men exchange the images of fire and water. Blood and choler (or anger) dominate the early struggles between the two men. Then, as Bullingbrook rises, so Richard takes on the wet and cold qualities of phlegm and finally, like the humour of melancholy, finds his resting place in the cold, dry earth.

These elemental images are perhaps most insistent in the opening scenes and at the crucial moment of change. Read 1.1, 3.2, 3.3 and 4.1, noting the occurrence of images of earth, air, fire, water, blood and choler. Devise a chart or diagram to show how they change and fluctuate.

Negatives

King Richard, in 4.1.219, calls himself 'unkinged Richard'. There are a number of such negative verbs (apparently Shakespeare's own inventions) in this play, all of which help give the play its reversible and contradictory quality. See if you can find some of the others. Try 2.1, 3.1, 3.2, 5.1 and 5.5.

Symphonic imagery

Music is heard just at the moment of deepest sympathy for Richard (5.5.41) but many people feel that the whole play resembles a complex piece of music where words, like melodies, fade in and out, appear, disappear and reappear, perhaps changed or modified but still recognisably part of the pattern.

Find three or four places where the following word-themes occur and decide how they help to express some of the preoccupations of the play. Each word-theme has a one line reference to get you started:

sweet and sour (1.3.235)
beggary, bankruptcy (4.1.308)
tears and weeping (1.4.5)
face (1.1.195)
gardens and growing (5.6.46)
blots, stains and washing (1.3.201)
plague, pestilence, infection (5.1.58–9)
hollowness, shadows (2.2.23).

Language, thought and reality

This is a vast philosophical question, but the play does present us with some interesting insights. Language is yet another word-theme running through the play (e.g. tongue, word, breath, throat, air, name). Words seem uncertain and unstable. Some characters hide behind them. Others use them to manipulate others or deceive themselves. The duchess says Gloucester's death was butchery, while the gardener calls it necessary pruning. Who sees the truth?

Read 1.3.207–14 and 252–308. Bullingbrook seems to think that reality should dominate language and thought, whereas for Richard it is words that dominate – they have a fatal fascination for him. This can be seen most spectacularly in the conceits he uses (pages 110 and 174). Read 3.2, 3.3 and 4.1. Look carefully at the way Richard uses and responds to words. In particular, read 3.3.172–85. Richard foresees in his descent to the base court his actual downfall. What does Northumberland unwittingly say which prompts him to think this?

Yet, strangely enough, it is this very 'weakness' which leads Richard ultimately to a deeper understanding and sympathy (5.5.1–66) while the pragmatic Bullingbrook becomes ever more silent.

Shakespeare's verse

Shakespeare wrote in blank verse because it worked. Modern actors say that it makes learning the lines easier and helps them shape their thoughts and phrasing. It has a powerful rhythmic flow and is more concise, particular and exact than prose.

There is nothing mysterious or difficult about blank verse. It is a verse form patterned very closely on the natural rhythms of English speech and may be defined as 'unrhymed lines made up of five pairs of light and strong stresses (**iambic pentameter**)':

I think I'll go and have a cup of tea

or (to use one from *King Richard II*):

'The blood is hot that must be cooled for this'.

Regular blank verse tends to pause at the end of each line ('end-stopping') and have a mid-line pause ('caesura'). These features can powerfully convey the balances and contrasts in the play. Read aloud 4.1.203–09. How do the caesuras and end-stops echo the dramatic situation at that moment? (see also pages 46, 56, 110 and 138)

Alternatively, one verse line can 'flow' into the next ('enjambement' or run-on line). Read aloud 3.2.54–62 and count the run-on lines. What kind of power does this more fluid structure give to Richard's speech? (see also page 96)

Shakespeare gets his effects by the way he both uses and rings the changes on these rhythmic patterns. The blank verse structure sets up a rhythmic pattern and energy and, when that basic rhythm is changed or broken, other often quite striking effects are created. You will already have discovered some of these from your work on different scenes.

Short lines can quicken or break the rhythm while others may have an extra syllable. Occasionally there are lines with an extra two syllables (termed an 'alexandrine'). What dramatic effect does York's alexandrine (2.3.167) create?

Formality and ceremony

King Richard II, unlike most of Shakespeare's plays, is written entirely in verse (largely blank verse but about one fifth in rhyme). This is very much in keeping with the ceremony and formality of the great events taking place on stage. The play is full of set speeches: declarations, statements of policy, prophecies of disaster, ceremonial actions, denunciations, persuasive speeches. Read the following examples aloud: Carlisle's denunciation and prophecy (4.1.114–49), Bulling-brook's challenge to Mowbray (1.1.69–77) and the gardener's speech (3.4.54–66). What different kinds of formality are there?

Rhymes and couplets

Rhymes can also enhance the formality and ceremony of a situation in subtle and complex ways (see page 152). Go through 1.1 just speaking the final word in each line so that you hear the rhyming couplets. Why do they occur where they do?

You will have noticed that a final couplet signals the end of a scene. Look at 1.2.44–74. How do the couplets also help suggest the duchess's hesitation?

Flexibility and variation

Read aloud York's agitated speech (2.2.103–21). How different in rhythm and structure are these lines compared to the basic blank verse pattern? Another variation used in the play is the shared line. What is the dramatic effect of line 2.2.147?

Above all there is the subtlety and variety of Richard's emotions. Match these descriptions of Richard's moods to the appropriate lines from the play:

1	fanciful poetry	a	2.1.115–23
2	cruel petulance	b	1.3.125–43
3	sad self-awareness	c	3.2.6–22
4	nervous irony	d	3.3.189–94
5	regal confidence	e	4.1.227–41
6	painful dignity	f	5.5.31–41.

William Shakespeare 1564–1616

1564 Born Stratford-upon-Avon, eldest son of John and Mary Shakespeare.
1582 Married to Anne Hathaway of Shottery, near Stratford.
1583 Daughter, Susanna, born.
1585 Twins, son and daughter, Hamnet and Judith, born.
1592 First mention of Shakespeare in London. Robert Greene, another playwright, described Shakespeare as 'an upstart crow beautified with our feathers . . .'. Greene seems to have been jealous of Shakespeare. He mocked Shakespeare's name, calling him 'the only Shake-scene in a country'. (presumably because Shakespeare was writing successful plays).
1595 A shareholder in 'The Lord Chamberlain's Men', an acting company that became extremely popular.
1596 Son Hamnet died, aged 11.
   Father, John, granted arms (acknowledged as a gentleman).
1597 Bought New Place, the grandest house in Stratford.
1598 Acted in Ben Jonson's *Every Man in His Humour*.
1599 Globe Theatre opens on Bankside. Performances in the open air.
1601 Father, John, dies.
1603 James I granted Shakespeare's company a royal patent: 'The Lord Chamberlain's Men' became 'The King's Men' and played about twelve performances each year at court.
1607 Daughter, Susanna, marries Dr John Hall.
1608 Mother, Mary, dies.
1609 'The King's Men' begin performing indoors at Blackfriars Theatre.
1610 Probably returned from London to live in Stratford.
1616 Daughter, Judith, marries Thomas Quiney.
   Died. Buried in Holy Trinity Church, Stratford-upon-Avon.

The plays and poems

(no one knows exactly when he wrote each play)

1589–1595 *The Two Gentlemen of Verona, The Taming of the Shrew, First, Second and Third Parts of King Henry VI, Titus Andronicus, King Richard III, The Comedy of Errors, Love's Labour's Lost, A Midsummer Night's Dream, Romeo and Juliet, King Richard II* (and the long poems *Venus and Adonis* and *The Rape of Lucrece*).

1596–1599 *King John, The Merchant of Venice, First and Second Parts of King Henry IV, The Merry Wives of Windsor, Much Ado About Nothing, King Henry V, Julius Caesar* (and probably the *Sonnets*).

1600–1605 *As You Like It, Hamlet, Twelfth Night, Troilus and Cressida, Measure for Measure, Othello, All's Well That Ends Well, Timon of Athens, King Lear.*

1606–1611 *Macbeth, Antony and Cleopatra, Pericles, Coriolanus, The Winter's Tale, Cymbeline, The Tempest.*

1613 *King Henry VIII, The Two Noble Kinsmen* (both probably with John Fletcher)

1623 Shakespeare's plays published as a collection (now called the First Folio).